Money Skills
for Teens and Young Adults

Money Skills
for Teens and Young Adults

A Fast Track to Financial Savvy:
Learn to Budget, Save Wisely, Invest Smartly, Spend Prudently, and Secure Your Future in Just 15 Minutes a Day

Freddie Awuah-Gyasi

All rights reserved. No part of this publication or its characters may be reproduced, distributed, or transmitted in any form or by any means, including photocopying, recording, or other electronic or mechanical methods, without the prior written permission of the publisher, except in the case of brief quotations embodied in reviews and certain other noncommercial uses permitted by copyright law.

PaperBack: 979-8-9904416-1-3

Hardback: 979-8-9904416-2-0

Ebook: 979-8-9904416-0-6

©2024 Copyright Freddie Awuah-Gyasi

All Rights Reserved

Printed in the United States of America

To the bright young minds of today and the leaders of tomorrow, and to the parents and future parents guiding them through life's financial journeys, and for you—the dreamers, innovators, and change-makers, and the dedicated guardians fostering their growth.

May you always be courageous in your queries, strong in your pursuit of knowledge, and wise in its application.

To my family, whose unwavering support and love illuminate my path, thank you. This journey would have been incomplete without you.

TABLE OF CONTENTS

Introduction 9

CHAPTER 1:
Building a Strong Financial Foundation 15

CHAPTER 2:
Unlocking Your Earning Potential 41

CHAPTER 3:
Your Journey through Banking 67

CHAPTER 4:
Budgeting Mastery 89

CHAPTER 5:
Saving for a Rainy Day 105

CHAPTER 6:
Crafting a Wise Spending Blueprint 121

CHAPTER 7:
Wealth Building Made Easier 135

CHAPTER 8:
Navigating Debt and Credit Scores 151

CHAPTER 9:
Retire Rich, Retire Happy 167

CONCLUSION 183

ACKNOWLEDGMENTS 186
ABOUT THE AUTHOR 187
REFERENCES 189
INDEX 191

INTRODUCTION

Did you know that 87% of teenagers in the United States feel lost when it comes to managing their finances? This startling statistic isn't just a number–it reflects a reality faced by young adults like you. It's time for a change, and ***Money Skills for Teens and Young Adults: A Fast Track to Financial Savvy*** is your first step toward that transformation, as it's our goal to ensure you're not part of these statistics.

Imagine standing at the entrance of a financial maze, your heart racing as you realize that every turn inside could lead you closer to, or further away from, your dreams. There is the road of endless bills, winding and unpredictable, and the path of impulsive spending, deceptively inviting. Then there is the daunting trail of savings and investments, shrouded in misty uncertainty. In this maze, each step feels like a gamble, and each decision has heavy consequences. If this mental image makes your pulse quicken, if you've ever felt lost in the complexities of managing money, then you're in the right place at the right moment.

I've stood at these crossroads, feeling that pulse of anxiety with every financial decision. There was a time when the balance in my bank account seemed like a foreign language—complex, and incomprehensible. The journey from there to here, from confusion to clarity, wasn't just a path I walked, it was a transformation I lived. Are you ready to embark on this journey?

Welcome to a book that doesn't just talk about money but actually breathes life into your financial dreams. This isn't about dry numbers or abstract theories—it's about turning your financial fears into milestones of success. Let's navigate this maze together, transforming each challenge into a stepping stone toward your financial independence.

The Power of 15 Minutes
Transforming Your Financial Life, One Quarter-Hour at a Time

Imagine what can be achieved in just 15 minutes a day—that's less time than you spend scrolling through social media. This book introduces a revolutionary 15-minute daily routine designed to be seamlessly integrated into your busy life. Each day, these bite-sized lessons build upon each other, transforming your understanding and management of

INTRODUCTION

money without overwhelming you. These 15 minutes are your daily investment in a future of financial freedom and stability.

The Practical Toolkit

We dive deep into interactive exercises, step-by-step guides, and real-life case studies. These tools are designed to resonate with your life, offering practical applications for your unique financial situation. Whether it's setting up your first budget, understanding how to save for your goals, or navigating the world of credit and debt, this book translates complex financial concepts into clear, actionable steps.

Technology at Your Fingertips

In an era where digital banking and social media are at the forefront of financial trends, this book guides you on leveraging technology for your financial benefit. Learn how to use apps and online resources to make informed financial decisions, aligning modern tools with your financial goals.

The Future is Yours

This book is designed to help you jumpstart your personal journey into transforming challenges into growth opportunities. It's about shifting from financial confusion to clarity and confidence. By mastering the skills taught here, you embark on a path to financial independence, equipped to make decisions that align with your personal and financial aspirations.

Interactive Learning at Its Best
Engage, Apply, and Master

Dive into interactive exercises that mirror real-life financial scenarios. These aren't hypothetical situations but practical challenges you face every day. Whether it's budgeting with your part-time job income or planning for college expenses, the book's activities are designed for hands-on learning, ensuring that the concepts stick.

A Testimonial That Speaks Volumes
From Financial Chaos to Clarity: A Reader's Journey
Meet Alex, a college sophomore who once felt overwhelmed by mounting debt and limited income. "This book was a game-changer for me," Alex shares. "The 15-minute daily routine was surprisingly doable and incredibly effective. It turned my financial chaos into a structured plan that I could confidently follow.

Personalized Pathways
Because we recognize the diversity among our readers, this book offers various pathways to financial savvy. Whether you're a high school student saving for your first car, a college student navigating part-time work, or a young adult planning for your first major investment, there are tailored strategies for everyone. This personalized approach ensures that you will find relevant and practical advice regardless of your financial journey.

A Commitment to Your Future
This book is not just about immediate financial gains—it's about laying the groundwork for a prosperous future. By instilling sound financial habits now, you're setting yourself up for long-term success. Think of this as planting a seed that will grow into a sturdy tree, providing shade and security for years to come.

INTRODUCTION

Let's be honest, the path to financial savvy comes with challenges. There will be moments of doubt, temptation, and setbacks. But remember, this book is more than just a guide—it's a companion for those moments. Together, we will sail through these challenges, turning them into learning experiences and stepping stones to greater achievements.

Meet Your Guide: Freddie Awuah-Gyasi

As your guide on this journey to financial literacy, I, Freddie Awuah-Gyasi, am here to share not just my academic knowledge, but also the wisdom gained from real-life experiences. At 38, a father of three, and deeply committed to my faith, my personal finance approach is grounded in family life and a strong academic foundation.

My passion for financial education is driven by personal experiences and a deep desire to prepare the next generation for financial success. My teachings, covering budgeting, saving, and investing, are practical and resonate with the real-life challenges you face.

As a parent, I understand the importance of starting financial education early, and I bring this perspective into every page of my writing. My goal is to inspire and empower you to take control of your financial future confidently. This book, along with my workshops and speaking engagements, is part of my mission to spread financial literacy among young people. I'm here to guide you every step of the way.

Begin Your Journey to Financial Savvy

As you turn each page of *Money Skills for Teens and Young Adults*, remember that this is more than just a guide—it's a journey toward empowerment. This book is your starting point for a future where financial literacy is a tool for personal success and stability. It's time to take control of your financial destiny, to turn your challenges into milestones of success. Your journey to financial independence starts now. Join us, and together, let's unlock the doors to your financial empowerment.

CHAPTER 1:

BUILDING A STRONG FINANCIAL FOUNDATION

"*Money grows on the tree of persistence.*" — THIS JAPANESE PROVERB encapsulates the essence of our journey through the world of finance. As we embark on this adventure, let's delve into the realities of the financial landscape facing teens and young adults today. You're not just opening a book—you're unlocking a treasure chest of knowledge, wisdom, and practical advice to navigate the tumultuous seas of personal finance.

Financial Challenges of Young Adults and Teens

In the vibrant hustle of youth, financial hurdles often lurk in the shadows, waiting to trip you up. But fear not! I'm here, your trusty guide, to shine a light on these challenges and equip you with the tools to overcome them.

Financial Illiteracy: It's like being in a foreign country where you don't speak the language. The world of finance can seem bewildering, with its jargon and complexity. This book is your Rosetta Stone, decoding the language of money and transforming confusion into clarity.

Debt - The Sneaky Frenemy: It's easy to fall into the clutches of debt, be it through credit cards, student loans, or personal borrowing. Think of debt as a sneaky frenemy - it can seem helpful but can stab you in the back if you're not careful. Here, you'll learn the art of managing and conquering debt, turning a potential enemy into a stepping stone.

Financial Fragility - Walking on Thin Ice: Living paycheck to paycheck is like skating on thin ice—one wrong move, and you're in cold water. We'll explore how to thicken that ice with savings strategies and emergency funds, giving you a solid ground to stand on.

The Missing Piece - Lack of a Financial Plan: Have you ever tried assembling a jigsaw puzzle without the picture on the box? That's what navigating finances without a plan feels like. Together, we'll piece together your financial puzzle, creating a picture of stability and prosperity.

Spending More than Earning - The Slippery Slope: It's tempting to live in the moment, splurging without a second thought. But unchecked spending is a slippery slope leading to financial quicksand. Fear not, for you'll learn how to balance life's pleasures with prudent spending.

The Elusive Safety Net - Not Having Savings: Imagine a trapeze artist performing without a safety net. That's you without savings. I'll show you how to weave your safety net, ensuring that you land safely when life throws you off balance.

Navigate Your Way to Financial Empowerment

You're not alone on this journey. Within these pages lie the solutions to these challenges. We'll embark on this voyage together, with me, Freddie Awuah-Gyasi, as your captain. I've navigated these waters before, and I'll guide you through every twist and turn.

This chapter is your first step toward financial empowerment. It's about laying the foundation stones of knowledge upon which you'll build your financial empire. We'll transform obstacles into stepping stones and confusion into confidence.

So gear up, young adventurer! With each page, you're not just reading—you're re-writing your financial story. Let's set sail toward a future where you're the master of your financial destiny, steering your ship toward the shores of prosperity and success.

Introduction to Money

"Rule No.1: Never lose money. **Rule No.2:** Never forget Rule No.1." Warren Buffett wasn't just throwing words around when he said this. Money, folks, isn't just green paper with dead presidents on it. It's the lifeblood of our modern world, the fuel for our dreams, and, sometimes, a tough master. But what exactly is this thing we hustle for day and night?

What's Money?: Picture money as the ultimate shape-shifter. In the old days, it was shells and beads. Today, it's paper, coins, and even digital digits. Essentially, money is an agreed-upon symbol, a tool that represents value. It's the golden key that unlocks the doors to just about anything you need or want. From a teen saving up for their first car to an entrepreneur investing in their next big venture, money is the silent character in everyone's story.

The Functions of Money: Money wears many hats, and understanding these roles is like decoding the DNA of finance. Let's break it down:

- **As a Medium of Exchange:** Here's the deal: Money is the universal middleman. Back in the day, if you wanted a cow, you had to find someone who wanted your 100 chickens. Enter money, the hero of the story. It makes sure you don't have to haul livestock to the market to get what you need. Money acts as an accepted intermediary, making transactions smoother than a cold brew on a hot day.

- **As a Measure of Value:** Money is like the ruler of the economic world. Without it, determining the value of goods and services would be as confusing as a chameleon in a bag of Skittles. Money gives us a way to assign value, making it clear how much something is worth. It's the universal language of trade, speaking for everything from a candy bar to a mansion.

- **As a Store of Value:** Ever tried storing a year's supply of fish for future use? Doesn't work out well. Money, on the other hand, can be stashed for future needs without turning foul. It's a storage unit for purchasing power. Sure, inflation can nibble away at its value over time, but money allows you to save and plan for bigger dreams down the road. It's like a financial time capsule, preserving your economic power until you're ready to unleash it.

How is Money Created? "Show me the money!" Jerry Maguire wasn't just screaming about dollar bills; he was onto something deeper—the creation of money. Let's dive into this. Money doesn't just grow on trees (if only, right?). It's a sophisticated dance of economics and trust. Central banks, like the Federal Reserve in the U.S. or the Bank of England, are the DJs spinning the tracks here. They control the money supply, pumping out the dough in response to the economy's beats.

Picture this: A bank lends money. Boom! New money is created. It's like magic, but it's economics. Every time a bank issues a loan and someone takes it, the money supply expands. It's not just printing cash—it's about credit, loans, and digital dollars zooming across cyberspace. This system keeps the wheels of the economy greased, but too much oil and we slip into inflation; too little, and we're stuck in recession-ville.

A Brief History of Money: "Money is a tool of exchange, which can't exist unless there are goods produced and men able to produce them,"

Ayn Rand once said. Money's history is a blockbuster saga of human innovation. We started with bartering—"I'll trade my woolly mammoth steak for your firewood." Then we upped the game with coins made from precious metals, making trading as easy as flipping a coin.

But carrying a sack of coins? Not cool. Enter paper money—lightweight, easy, and backed by gold (initially). Fast forward, and now we're in the digital age. The new kids on the block are plastic cards, online transactions, and cryptocurrencies. Money has gone from tangible to virtual, proving it's not about the material but the value it represents.

So, always remember: Money's more than just what's in your wallet. It's a symbol, a tool, and a story—one that's been unfolding since the dawn of civilization. Strap in—this history is just part of your financial literacy saga. Let's make history while learning it!

What is Currency?

Alright, let's talk currency—the MVP of the financial game. Think of currency as the universal language of buying and selling. It's the bridge between what you've got and what you want. In simpler terms, currency is the physical form of money—the tangible stuff you stash in your wallet, drop into piggy banks, or use to make it rain. It's the real deal, authorized by the government, giving it the street cred to be accepted everywhere, from swanky boutiques to your corner store.

Imagine going to a concert—the ticket you hold is your access pass. Similarly, currency is your all-access pass in the marketplace. It's more than just paper and metal; it's a ticket to trade, purchase, and exchange. As Biggie Smalls put it, "Mo Money, Mo Problems," but without this currency, you'd have even bigger problems!

BUILDING A STRONG FINANCIAL FOUNDATION

Types of Currency

Coins: Coins are like the durable, no-fuss veterans of currency. Made of metal, they jingle in your pockets and last longer than your favorite jeans. Each coin's got a value, a story, and sometimes, a bit of history stamped on it. From paying for a parking meter to making wishes in a fountain, coins are the unsung heroes of small transactions.

Bills: Bills, or banknotes, are the flashy players in the currency team. They're lighter, easier to carry, and come in different colors and designs. Bills make handling larger sums a breeze. They're like those cool friends who are always welcome, whether at a fancy dinner or a quick coffee run.

Plastic Money: Today, plastic money—credit and debit cards—reigns supreme. It's like having a financial wizard in your pocket. A swipe here, a tap there, and transactions are smoother than a slick TikTok dance.

Plastic money links your bank to your buys, making shopping sprees or online splurges a walk in the park. It's the new-age financial wand, turning digital numbers into real stuff.

How to Count Money

Alright, let's break it down: counting money. It's not just about knowing your numbers—it's about being street-smart with your cash. Think of it like a DJ mixing tracks—you've got to blend different beats, or in this case, bills and coins, to make the perfect tune. Here's the lowdown on how to count your dough like a pro.

First up, separate your bills and coins. Like sorting your playlist, you gotta know what goes where. Line up those bills from the big ballers (higher values) to the little guys (lower values). Do the same with your coins—quarters, dimes, nickels, and then pennies.

Now, start with the coins. Count up each group, starting from the highest value. Add 'em up until you hit the dollar mark, then shift to the next set. Keep it rolling until all your coins are counted.

Next, hit the bills. Again, start from the top. Stack 'em up, count 'em out. Each bill is a step closer to knowing your total worth.

Finally, combine your coin and bill totals. That's your grand total. It's like hitting the jackpot on a slot machine – ding, ding, ding!

Pro tip: Always double-check your count. Better safe than sorry, right?

Counting money is like playing a game of Tetris. You've got to fit each piece in the right place. Master this skill, and you're on your way to being the maestro of your financial orchestra. Keep it cool, keep it accurate, and watch your financial skills level up!

Can Money Buy Happiness?

"Money can't buy happiness, but it's a lot more comfortable to cry in a Mercedes than on a bicycle." Let's face it, money talks, but can it sing the tune of happiness? Here's the deal: Money isn't a magic wand for joy, but it sure does give you options. It's like having VIP passes to life's concert. With money, you can grab experiences, comfort, and opportunities that might otherwise be out of reach.

But here's the twist: It's not just about the cash in your pocket—it's about how you use it. Splurging on the latest iPhone or designer gear might give you a quick high, but it's like fast food for the soul—feels good now, but doesn't really nourish you. Real happiness? That's more about experiences, relationships, and a sense of achievement.

Money can set the stage for happiness—think stability, freedom, and the ability to pursue your passions. It can remove barriers and open doors. But the show's real star is the way you live your life and your choices. It's about finding joy in both the journey and the destination.

So, can money buy happiness? It can rent it for sure. But for true, lasting happiness, that's on you. Use your money as a tool, not a crutch. Invest in experiences, in people, and in your dreams. That's where the real happiness lies—in a life well-lived, not just well-funded.

Why is Money Important?

"Money is a terrible master but an excellent servant." – P.T. BARNUM wasn't just talking circus when he said this. In the grand circus of life, money plays a ringmaster of sorts. Let's break down why money isn't just important—it's essential, especially for you, the savvy teens and young adults ready to take on the world.

Freedom and Control: First off, money is like the ultimate backstage pass. It gives you access to choices, freedoms, and control over your life that you just can't get otherwise. Want to jet off on a spontaneous adventure? Money's got you covered. Dreaming of starting your own gig? Money is the fuel for your entrepreneurial rocket. It's about living life on your terms, not at the mercy of circumstances.

The Power of Choice: Picture money as your personal Spotify playlist—it gives you the option to choose your tunes. From deciding where you live, to what you eat, to which college you attend, money puts you in the DJ booth. It's the difference between "I have to" and "I choose to." Money turns life's volume up, giving you the power to dance to your beat.

Pursuing Your Passion: Here's the real kicker: Money can help turn passions into paychecks. Love painting? Money buys those canvases and oils. Got a thing for coding? Money gets you that killer laptop and software. It's not just about making a living—it's about making a life doing what you love. Money is the ticket to the passion party.

Security Blanket: Ever tried sleeping peacefully on a bed of uncertainty? Doesn't work. Money is like that cozy security blanket. It's knowing your bills are paid, your fridge is full, and you're not one emergency away from a meltdown. Financial security means fewer sleepless nights and more peace of mind. It's not about hoarding wealth Scrooge-style, but about having that cushion to fall back on.

Shift Your Mindset in a Few Steps

Ready to shift gears in your financial journey? It's all about your mindset. Like a skilled driver on a winding road, your success with money largely depends on how you navigate the twists and turns. Let's dive into tweaking that mindset, transforming it from a bumpy road into a smooth highway toward financial freedom.

What's a Money Mindset? Think of a money mindset as your financial fingerprint—it's unique to you. It's the set of beliefs and attitudes you carry around about money. This mindset shapes how you view earning, spending, saving, and investing. Like a pair of glasses, it colors everything you see in finance. Got a mindset that sees opportunities? You'll find them. Stuck in a mindset that whispers 'money is evil' or 'I'll never be rich'? That's a rocky road, my friend.

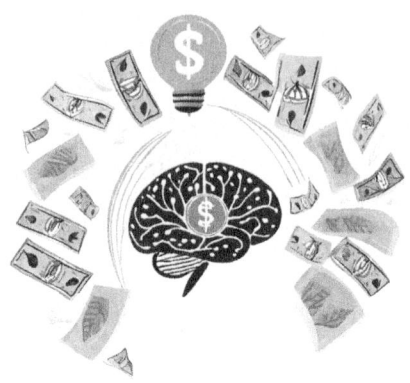

How is a Money Mindset Formed?

Now, let's unpack how this mindset comes into being. It's not just plucked from thin air—it's crafted over time, influenced by a cocktail of experiences and teachings.

The Psychology of Money Itself: Money isn't just paper and coins—it's loaded with emotional and psychological baggage. It represents power, security, freedom, and sometimes, even fear and envy. How you perceive money shapes your interactions with it.

Your Personal Financial Experiences: Every dollar earned, spent, saved, or lost tells a story. These experiences, whether they're triumphs or setbacks, lay the bricks of your financial mindset.

Your Financial Journey Growing Up: The way money flowed (or didn't flow) in your household sets the stage. Were your guardians spendthrifts or savers? Did money discussions echo with stress or with strategic planning? These early imprints leave lasting marks.

Your Parents/Guardians' View About Money: Ever heard the phrase, "Monkey see, monkey do"? Well, we often mirror our guardians' money habits and attitudes. Whether healthy or not, their approach to finances often becomes our starting point.

Understanding your money mindset is like holding a map. It shows you where you are and how you got there. And it can help chart a course to where you want to be. In the following sections, we'll explore how to navigate this map, steering your mindset toward a destination of financial well-being and savvy. Let's rev up those engines!

Why It's Important to Understand Your Money Mindset

You've heard it a million times: "Mind over money!" But let's break down why understanding your money mindset isn't just cool advice—it's critical for financial swagger. Your money mindset is like the GPS in your financial journey. If it's set to "Lost in Money Misery," guess where you're heading? Straight to Brokesville. But, switch it to "Abundance Avenue," and you're on your way to prosperity city.

Understanding your money mindset is like having X-ray vision. It lets you see through those sneaky subconscious beliefs that secretly steer your financial decisions. Ever wondered why some folks are like Midas, turning everything to gold, while others couldn't catch a financial break if it landed in their lap? That's mindset magic, folks.

Types of Money Mindset

The Poor Mindset / Scarcity Mindset: The scarcity mindset is like wearing "pessimist glasses." Everything looks limited, including money. Think of it as living in a financial horror movie, where every dollar is a potential scare. This mindset whispers lies like "Money doesn't grow on trees," or "You've got to hoard what you have." It's like being in a perpetual state of financial drought, constantly worried that the money well is about to run dry.

The Rich Mindset / Abundance Mindset: Now, flip the script to the abundance mindset. This is where the party's at. It's seeing life as a buffet of financial opportunities. The abundance mindset is all about believing that there's plenty of wealth to go around, and you're just as entitled to a piece of the pie as anyone else. It's about thinking big, dreaming big, and expecting big. It's not about being reckless with cash; it's about smart, confident choices. This mindset sees money as a tool, not a trap. It's a sunny day in the world of finance.

Why This Matters: Getting cozy with your money mindset is like having a heart-to-heart with your financial future. It's about understanding the "why" behind your money moves. This understanding is your ticket to change. It's the secret sauce to rewriting your financial story from "tragic" to "epic".

So, as you cruise through *Money Skills for Teens and Young Adults,* keep your mind open. We're not just talking numbers and budgets; we're talking beliefs and attitudes. We're digging deep, uprooting those sneaky, unhelpful thoughts, and planting seeds of financial confidence and know-how.

Remember, your money mindset isn't just about the green in your wallet—it's about the ideas in your head. And once you get those right, the sky's the limit. Let's transform that mindset and watch your bank account thank you for it. Time to flip the switch and light up your financial future!

Money Skills for Life - Financial Literacy

Now when you are in the big league, you must understand that financial literacy isn't just a fancy term—it's your secret weapon in the game of life. Think of money skills as your financial toolkit. Just as a mechanic needs the right tools to fix a car, you need the right skills to manage your cash. It's about being the boss of your bucks, not letting the bucks boss you around.

What are Money Skills? Money skills are like the cheat codes to the financial game. They're a mix of know-how, street smarts, and savvy that help you handle your cash like a pro. Let's break it down:

• **Budgeting - Your Financial Blueprint:** It's about planning where your money should go instead of wondering where it went. Budgeting is like setting up a GPS for your finances. You input your destination (financial goals), and it maps out the best route (spending plan).

• **Saving - Your Financial Safety Net:** Saving money is like building your own financial fort. It's there to protect you when life throws curveballs. It's not just about stashing cash for a rainy day—it's about giving future you a helping hand.

- **Investing – Let Your Money Hustle for You:** Investing is how you turn your savings into more money. It's like planting a seed and watching it grow into a money tree. Stocks, bonds, real estate—it's all about making your money work harder than a caffeinated beaver.

- **Understanding Debt – Not All Debt is the Devil:** Debt can be a tool or a trap. Knowing how to use debt wisely, like for education or a mortgage, can be a game changer. But beware of the debt traps, like high-interest credit cards, that can sink your financial ship.

- **Smart Spending – Spend Like a Pro, Not a Rookie:** Smart spending is about making your dollars do the heavy lifting. It's not about being cheap; it's about spending on what truly matters to you and cutting out the financial fluff.

- **Financial Planning – Plotting Your Financial Future:** This is about setting long-term goals, like buying a house or retiring while you're still young enough to enjoy it. It's your financial road trip map, and you're in the driver's seat.

- **Credit Management – Keeping Your Credit in Check:** Good credit can open doors, like getting a loan for that startup you dream of. It's about understanding credit scores and how to keep yours as shiny as a new penny.

- **Risk Management – Don't Let Life's Surprises Wipe You Out:** It's about being ready for life's what-ifs. Insurance, emergency funds, diversifying investments—it's all about not putting all your financial eggs in one basket.

The Importance of Mastering Money Skills

Let's get real, folks! Mastering money skills is like having a superpower in today's world. It's not just about making bank but making your bank work for you. Financial literacy is the Swiss army knife in your life's toolbox, and here's why it's more crucial than that morning cup of coffee:

Navigating the Maze of Needs and Wants: Money skills help you play the ultimate game of "Would You Rather." Would you rather splurge on that flashy new phone or save up for college? It's about distinguishing between the "gotta haves" and the "nice-to-haves." Mastering this skill is like having a financial compass—it always points you toward smart decisions, keeping you from getting lost in the forest of impulse buys.

Breeding Responsibility – Welcome to the Real World: Let's face it—handling money responsibly is like adulting 101. It teaches you the value of hard work, the power of delayed gratification, and the art of prioritizing. Every dollar you manage wisely is a step toward becoming more responsible and independent. It's like leveling up in life.

Empowerment - Your Financial Cape: Knowing your way around finances is empowering. It's like having a secret weapon against life's curveballs. With financial literacy, you're no longer at the mercy of confusing jargon, intimidating bank meetings, or perplexing tax forms. You become the captain of your financial ship, confidently navigating the waters of money matters.

Cultivating Healthy Financial Habits - Planting Seeds for Future Wealth: Good money habits are like seeds—plant them early, and you'll reap a harvest of wealth and stability. Budgeting, saving, investing—these aren't just buzzwords; they're habits that shape your financial future. Just like eating your veggies and hitting the gym, these habits ensure a healthy, prosperous life—financially speaking.

Important Money Skills to Master

In the arena of life, money skills are your armor, your shield, and your battle strategy. This isn't just about counting coin—it's about mastering the art of making your money work for you. So, let's dive into the key skills you need to be the financial warrior you were born to be.

Money Saving Skills - Your Financial Fortress: Saving money is like building your personal financial fortress. It's your defense against unexpected sieges like car repairs or sudden job losses. But here's the kicker: saving isn't just about stashing away cash; it's about being smart. It's knowing when to say, "Nah, I don't need that extra pair of sneakers" or "Maybe I'll cook at home instead of eating out." This book is your blueprint to build that fortress, brick by brick.

Investing Skills – Make Your Money Multiply: Investing is where the magic happens. It's turning your saved dollars into an army that fights to grow your wealth. But hey, it's not just throwing cash at the stock market and hoping for the best. It's about understanding risk, diversifying your portfolio, and playing the long game. Think of it as your financial chess game; every move should be calculated and strategic.

Making Money Skills – More Than a 9 to 5: Making money isn't confined to a dreary 9 to 5. It's about finding creative and effective ways to increase your income. Side hustles, freelance gigs, turning a hobby into a business— the possibilities are endless. This book isn't just about making a living; it's about making a killing.

Basic Budgeting – Your Financial Roadmap: Budgeting is the GPS of your financial journey. It tells you where your money should go so you don't end up lost in the land of Overspending. It's about setting limits that don't choke your fun but keep you on track toward your financial goals. Remember, a budget isn't a chain; it's a liberating plan that gives you control.

Dealing with Debt – Break Those Chains: Debt can feel like carrying a backpack full of bricks. But guess what? You have the power to lighten that load. Dealing with debt is about understanding interest rates, prioritizing payments, and knowing the difference between good debt (like a mortgage) and bad debt (like high-interest credit cards). This book is your guide to breaking those chains.

Building Strong Credit – Your Financial Reputation

Your credit score is like your financial reputation in the eyes of lenders. A strong credit score can open doors to lower interest rates and better loan terms. It's about paying bills on time, managing credit cards wisely, and keeping your credit utilization low. Think of it as your financial report card; you want those A's.

Interactive Element: What's Your Relationship with Money

Self-Assessment Quiz

Hey, Financial Trailblazers! Ready to uncover your money story? This self-assessment quiz is your golden ticket to understanding your relationship with money. Be real, be honest, and remember, no judgment here – we're all about growth and transformation. Take a minute on each question, dive deep, and let's unravel your financial narrative. Let the quiz begin!

1. **When you receive money (like a gift, salary, or bonus), what's your first instinct?**
    1. ☐ Save it immediately
    2. ☐ Spend it on something you've wanted
    3. ☐ Pay off debts or bills
    4. ☐ Invest it

2. **How often do you check your bank balance?**
    1. ☐ Every day, like clockwork
    2. ☐ Occasionally, when I remember
    3. ☐ Only when I need to make a transaction

4. ☐ I avoid it – it stresses me out

3. Growing up, how did your family talk about money?
    1. ☐ Openly and often, with advice and tips
    2. ☐ Rarely, it was a taboo topic
    3. ☐ In a stressed or negative way
    4. ☐ It wasn't really discussed much

4. What does money represent to you?
    1. ☐ Security and stability
    2. ☐ Freedom and choices
    3. ☐ Stress and anxiety
    4. ☐ Power and success

5. How do you feel about your current financial situation?
    1. ☐ Confident and in control
    2. ☐ It's okay, but I wish I had more
    3. ☐ Anxious and overwhelmed
    4. ☐ Indifferent or resigned

6. When making a big purchase, you tend to...
    1. ☐ Plan, research, and save for it
    2. ☐ Make an impulsive decision if you really want it
    3. ☐ Think about it for a long time and maybe never buy it
    4. ☐ Consult with others for advice

7. What's your approach to saving money?
    1. ☐ I have a solid savings plan and stick to it

2. ☐ I save occasionally, but not consistently
3. ☐ Saving? What's that?
4. ☐ I try, but something always comes up

8. Do you have a budget?
1. ☐ Yes, and I track every penny
2. ☐ A rough idea, but it's not strict
3. ☐ No, but I think I should
4. ☐ Budgets are too restrictive for me

9. How do you feel about investing your money?
1. ☐ Excited and informed about the possibilities
2. ☐ Interested, but not sure where to start
3. ☐ Nervous – it feels like a gamble
4. ☐ Not my thing – too complicated

10. When faced with a financial setback, you...
1. ☐ Adjust your budget and plan accordingly
2. ☐ Feel stressed but try to manage
3. ☐ Feel hopeless and avoid dealing with it
4. ☐ Borrow money or use credit to cope

11. What's your biggest financial fear?
1. ☐ Not having enough for retirement
2. ☐ Being stuck in debt
3. ☐ Losing my income source
4. ☐ Financial dependency

12. How often do you splurge on yourself?
1. ☐ Rarely, I'm quite frugal
2. ☐ Sometimes, if I feel I deserve it
3. ☐ Often, I live in the moment
4. ☐ Splurging makes me feel guilty

13. When it comes to financial advice, you…
1. ☐ Seek it actively from books, mentors, or courses
2. ☐ Get it from friends or family
3. ☐ Don't really look for it
4. ☐ Feel skeptical about financial advice

14. Your dream vacation is coming up. How do you plan for it financially?
1. ☐ Save up specifically for it months in advance
2. ☐ Use a bit of savings and some from the current income
3. ☐ Put it on a credit card and worry about it later
4. ☐ Vacations are a luxury I can't afford

15. How do you envision your financial future?
1. ☐ Optimistic and well-planned
2. ☐ Hopeful but uncertain
3. ☐ Worried and doubtful
4. ☐ Haven't really thought about it

Segue

Alright budgeting bosses, we've just cruised through some serious terrain in the world of financial literacy. Like any epic road trip, we've seen the highs, navigated the curves, and maybe even dodged a few potholes. But hey, that's what makes the journey thrilling, right?

We kicked off with a real talk about the financial challenges you face — the good, the bad, and the ugly. We dove deep into the nitty-gritty of what money really is, its history, and how it evolved from barter to Bitcoin. We even busted some myths about currency—because, let's face it, understanding your dough is key to making it grow.

But here's the kicker: We didn't just talk theory. Nope, we got our hands dirty with the real skills—the kind that turns a financial newbie into a money-savvy guru. We talked about saving like a pro, investing like a boss, and making money moves that would make even Robert Kiyosaki give us a nod of approval.

Now, as we hit the pause button (just for a moment, promise!), let's rewind and replay the highlights:

- Mastering the difference between needs and wants—because knowing when to splurge and when to save is a game-changer.
- Embracing financial responsibility—because adulting doesn't have to be a drag.
- The empowerment that comes with financial literacy—because knowledge is power, especially when it comes to your wallet.
- And let's not forget the healthy financial habits we're building—because good habits are the foundation of a wealthy future.

As we gear up for the next chapter, get ready to shift into a higher gear. We're going to tackle the art of shifting your money mindset. It's about transforming the way you think, feel, and interact with money. We're talking about going from a scarcity mindset, where every dollar feels like a battle, to an abundance mindset, where wealth flows as freely as the lyrics in a sick rap track.

Expect to dive into the nitty-gritty of different money mindsets—the poor mindset that holds you back, and the rich mindset that propels you forward. And because we're all about action, we'll equip you with the steps to start making that shift today. It's like getting the keys to a brand-new sports car—your financial freedom.

So, buckle up, financial adventurers! The next chapter is going to turbocharge your money mindset and set the stage for a lifetime of wealth, freedom, and success. Let's make "broke" a thing of the past and "wealthy" your new normal. Onward to financial greatness!

Interpreting your Results

Mostly 1s: The Savvy Saver
Mostly 2s: The Aspiring Optimist
Mostly 3s: The Cautious Navigator
Mostly 4s: The Reluctant Planner

Reflect on your quiz results as a starting point for growth. Whether you're a Savvy Saver, an Aspiring Optimist, a Cautious Navigator, or a Reluctant Planner, your financial persona is a window into your strengths and areas for development. Use these insights as a springboard to delve deeper into your financial capabilities and aspirations. Remember, this journey is about progression, not perfection. Each step you take is a step closer to mastering your money story.

Interpreting Your Financial Self:
Savvy Savers: Your prudence and planning are your superpowers. Embrace them, and consider venturing into new territories of investment and wealth building to stretch these abilities further.

Aspiring Optimists: Channel your positive energy into crafting structured financial strategies. Your optimism is your rocket fuel, and with the right tools and knowledge, the sky is the limit.

Cautious Navigators: Your caution is not a barrier but a solid foundation. Build upon it with education and actionable steps to transform your caution into a strategic financial advantage.

Reluctant Planners: Simplify the complexity and stress of financial planning by setting clear, achievable goals. Step by step, you'll find clarity and confidence in the financial landscape.

Bridging Insights to Action:
As we move forward to "Unlocking Your Earning Potential" in Chapter 2, remember that earning is about more than just money—it's about intention, strategy, and insight. Your journey through this quiz is just the beginning. Every aspect of your financial mindset, from saving and spending to planning and investing, plays a crucial role in shaping your earning potential. Let's navigate these financial seas with confidence, armed with the knowledge and skills to make your financial dreams a reality.

CHAPTER 2:

UNLOCKING YOUR EARNING POTENTIAL

Making money is a hobby that will complement any other hobbies you have beautifully. — SCOTT ALEXANDER

Meet Alex, 15, who transformed his digital art passion into a lucrative online business. Starting with custom designs for friends, his talent skyrocketed into high demand. By 16, he's earned over $500K. This isn't fiction—it's a testament to how age doesn't define financial success.

Making Money: It's More Than Just a Job

In this chapter, we will shift gears from just managing money to making it multiply. It's about breaking the mindset that earning is limited to a 9-5 job. We're talking about diverse income streams, side hustles, and turning hobbies into cash cows. It's time to tap into your inner entrepreneur and see money-making as a thrilling adventure.

The Art of Multiple Income Streams: Imagine having not just one but several faucets pouring money into your life. We're exploring the power of multiple income streams, from passive income like investments and royalties to active hustles like freelancing or a part-time gig. It's about creating a financial ecosystem where your money works as hard as you do.

The Entrepreneurial Spirit - Your Ticket to Financial Freedom: Here's where we inject some Robert Kiyosaki wisdom into the mix. Entrepreneurship isn't just about starting businesses—it's a mindset. It's about seeing opportunities where others see obstacles, taking risks, and innovating. Whether it's turning a passion for gaming into a YouTube channel or using your coding skills to develop apps, the entrepreneurial spirit is your golden ticket to financial freedom.

Harnessing Technology - The Digital Goldmine: In a world where a single tweet can make stocks soar, understanding the digital landscape is crucial. We're diving into how leveraging technology can amplify your earning potential. From e-commerce to social media marketing, the digital world is a treasure trove for exploring.

Money Making and Morals - Balancing the Scale: Let's get real—making money is great, but it's not just about the Benjamins. It's about doing it ethically, sustainably, and responsibly. We discuss balancing profit with principles, ensuring your journey to wealth doesn't compromise your values.

The Value of Work

In a world where financial independence is the ultimate goal, understanding the value of work is more crucial than ever. For teens and young adults, stepping into the world of earning is not just about pocket money; it's a rite of passage into adulthood, a foray into real-world experiences that textbooks can't teach. Let's break down why earning your own money through a job or entrepreneurship is a game-changer.

Earn Income: Let's start with the obvious: money. Earning your own income is empowering. It's the difference between asking for a few bucks and having your own stash. Whether it's from a part-time job or a small business venture, earning your own money opens doors. You can save for that new phone, contribute to household expenses, or start building that college fund. It's about having the financial freedom to make choices—a crucial step towards adulthood.

Appreciate Money More: When you earn your money, you value it more. It's no longer just a number on a screen or a bill handed over by parents—it's a symbol of your hard work and time. You start understanding the real cost of things—that designer sneaker isn't just $100; it's ten hours of work. This appreciation builds a healthier relationship with money, paving the way for smarter spending and saving habits.

Gradual Transformation into Adulthood: Getting a job or starting a business is like a trial run for adulthood. You learn to manage responsibilities, juggle schedules, and navigate the complexities of the working world. It's a safe space to make mistakes, learn, and grow. These experiences are invaluable as they lay the groundwork for a smooth transition into adult life, where responsibilities exponentially increase.

Learning the Value of Doing a Job Right: There's an old saying, "If a job is worth doing, it's worth doing well." Working teaches you just that. Whether it's flipping burgers with precision or coding a website meticulously, doing a job right is a lesson in excellence and work ethic. It's about taking pride in what you do, regardless of the task's nature. This mindset, when cultivated early, becomes a lifelong asset, setting you apart in both personal and professional realms.

Reinforcing Positive Values and Skills: The workplace is a melting pot of communication, teamwork, problem-solving, and time management lessons. These are not just job skills—they're life skills. A job reinforces the positive values and skills taught at home, like responsibility, punctuality, and respect for others. It's where you learn to work with different personalities, handle criticism constructively, and celebrate successes humbly.

How to Support Yourself Financially

In the bustling world of finances and future planning, a crucial skill often gets overshadowed—the art of supporting oneself financially. This isn't just about stacking cash but understanding the rhythm of income and expenses, dancing to a beat that ensures stability and growth.

As teens and young adults, you're on the cusp of a financial awakening. Gone are the days when piggy banks were your only financial worry. Now, it's about making smart choices with the money you earn, whether it's from a part-time gig, a summer internship, or that entrepreneurial venture you kicked off in your dorm room.

Money Moves: Smart Ways to Rock Your Earnings as a Teen or Young Adult

Alright, so you've got some cash flowing in—sweet! But here's where the real game begins. It's not just about earning—it's about mastering the art of using that money wisely. Here are some street-smart ways to make your money work for you:

Budget like a Boss: First things first, get a grip on budgeting. It's like having a map in a treasure hunt. Know where your money's going and plan for where you want it to go. There are cool apps out there to help you track your spending – use them!

Save for the Not-So-Sunny Days: Rainy day funds aren't just for adults. Start setting aside a small portion of your income. You never know when you might need some extra cash for an unexpected expense.

Invest in Your Future Self: Think of investments like planting a tree. It grows over time, and one day, it'll provide you with some sweet fruits. Whether it's stocks, bonds, or a small side business, start exploring.

Educate Yourself Financially: Knowledge is power, especially when it comes to money. Read up, attend workshops, or watch tutorials online. The more you know, the better you grow.

Crush those Debts Early: If you've got debts, make a plan to pay them off. The sooner you're debt-free, the sooner you can use your money for things that really matter.

Give Back: Earning money also gives you a chance to help others. Whether it's a charity, a cause you believe in, or helping out a friend in need, giving back is always in style.

Plan for Big Goals: Dreaming of a car, a world tour, or starting your own business? Start saving for these big goals. It's never too early to plan for your dreams.

Master the Art of Earning: Pro Strategies for Teens and Young Adults

Earning your own money is not just about filling your wallet—it's about shaping your future. In this digital age, where opportunities are as vast as your ambition, let's dive into the world of making money with a mix of old-school wisdom and new-age savvy.

- **Money Hacking 101: Quick and Clever Ways to Boost Your Bank Balance**

Earning money as a teen or young adult isn't just about mowing lawns or babysitting anymore. It's about leveraging the digital landscape and your unique skills. Here are some ingenious ways to get that cash flowing:

- **Monetize Your Social Media:** If you have a knack for creating content that resonates, social media platforms are your playground. You can turn your followers into dollars, from TikTok dances to Instagram stories.

- **Freelance Your Skills:** Good at graphic design, writing, or coding? Websites like Upwork and Fiverr are bustling with clients looking for your talent.

- **Online Tutoring:** Excel in a subject? Teach others online. Your knowledge can not only help others but also fill your pockets.

- **Sell Your Crafts:** Are you a DIY guru? Platforms like Etsy are ideal for selling your handmade goods.

- **Participate in Surveys and Tests:** Companies pay for your opinion. Sign up for online surveys and usability testing for websites.

Each of these tips represents a chance to learn, grow, and earn. It's about finding what suits you and turning it into an opportunity.

Job Hunt Like a Pro: Strategies for Securing Your First Gig

Landing your first job is a rite of passage. It's more than just earning—it's about stepping into the world of responsibility. Here's how to nail the job hunt:

Craft a Killer Resume: Your resume is your story. Make it compelling. Highlight your skills, volunteer work, and any relevant experience.

Network, Network, Network: Talk to family, friends, and teachers. Often, jobs come from people you know.

Leverage Social Media: Platforms like LinkedIn are not just for adults. Create a professional profile and connect with potential employers.

Prep for the Interview: First impressions count. Dress appropriately, arrive early, and practice answering common interview questions.

Follow Up: After the interview, send a thank-you email. It shows eagerness and professionalism.

Remember, getting a job is just the beginning. It's what you learn from it that truly counts. Be open, be eager, and let each job be a stepping stone to your next big adventure.

Cash In: Unleashing the Power of Online Earning

In a world where your smartphone is a gateway to opportunity, making money online isn't just a dream—it's your digital reality waiting to be tapped. Let's unlock the treasure trove of online income sources, blending caution with ambition, and setting you on a path to financial savvy.

- **Digital Goldmine: Your Guide to Making Money Online**

Ready to turn your online hours into dollars? Here's the lowdown on making it big in the virtual world while keeping it safe and smart:

- **Team Up with the 'Rents:** Loop in your folks. Whether it's setting up a PayPal account or vetting online job offers, their experience is your secret weapon.

- **Scam Alert:** The internet is wild, so watch out for sketchy offers.

Remember, if it sounds too good to be true, it probably is. No legit job will ask you to pay money upfront.

- **Safety First:** Guard your personal info like it's the last slice of pizza. Use secure passwords and don't share sensitive details with strangers online.

- **Career Prep Online:** Whether it's freelance writing, graphic designing, or coding, the internet is your playground to develop skills that can set the stage for your future career.

- **Tax Talk:** Uncle Sam's interested in your online success, too. Keep tabs on any earnings, as you might need to report them come tax time.

From selling your art on Etsy to tutoring math on Zoom, there's a world of opportunities waiting for you. So, dive in, be smart, and remember, every click can be a step toward your financial goals. Make it count!

The Digital Gold Rush: Unleashing Earnings in the Virtual World

The internet revolution has opened up many opportunities for digital earnings. From affiliate marketing to Twitch streaming, there are diverse ways to turn your online presence into a profitable venture. Here's a concise overview of some of the most popular methods:

Affiliate Marketing: Harness your passion and recommend products or services to earn commissions. It's all about connecting your audience with what they need or love through blogs, social media, or videos.

Dropshipping: Step into the e-commerce realm without the inventory stress. Set up an online store, market it effectively, and let the suppliers handle the rest.

Blogging: Your writing skills can become a steady income stream. Cover topics that fascinate you and monetize your blog through ads, sponsored content, or your products.

Twitch Streaming: For gaming enthusiasts, Twitch offers a platform to earn by engaging with a community of fellow passionate gamers. Income comes through subscriptions, donations, and sponsorships.

Game Boosting: If you're a skilled gamer, offer your expertise to help others level up in their favorite games for a fee.

A successful digital earning journey requires patience, persistence, and passion. Keep learning and adapting; you could be the next sensation in the vast digital landscape.

The Side Hustle: Rocking Part-time Jobs Like a Pro

Hey, future moguls and money maestros! Let's talk about the art of the side hustle. Part-time jobs aren't just about making a quick buck; they're your first steps in the dance of financial independence. So, let's dive into some kickin' part-time gigs that'll fatten your wallet and teach you skills that even money can't buy.

House Cleaning: Sparkle and Earn Roll up your sleeves because it's time to shine—literally. House cleaning isn't just about dust and dirte—it's an exercise in responsibility and efficiency. Plus, it pays! Whether it's helping neighbors or joining a local cleaning service, this job teaches you the value of hard work and gives your bank balance a nice polish.

Paid Internships: Earn While You Learn Imagine getting a sneak peek into your dream job while still filling your piggy bank. That's what paid internships are all about. They're like a double-decker bus—on one level, you're gaining real-world skills and networking like a boss, on the other, you're earning some cool cash. Start scouting for opportunities in fields you're curious about. It's like hitting two birds with one paycheck!

Food-Service Jobs: Serving Up Cash Restaurants, cafes, and diners are the classic arenas for part-time job gladiators. Whether you're flipping burgers, brewing coffee, or waiting tables, these jobs are a masterclass in time management, customer service, and teamwork. Plus, tips! Cha-ching! Wear your apron like armor and dive into the fast-paced world of food service.

Dog Walker: Cash and Cuddles Love dogs? Why not turn those cuddles into cash? Dog walking is not just a walk in the park; it's a responsibility—keep those furry friends happy and healthy. It's a great way to earn money, get some exercise, and learn about caring for another living being. Now, who wouldn't wag their tail to that?

Tutor Younger Students: Teach and Earn Got a knack for math, science, or any other subject? Put that brainpower to use by tutoring younger students. This gig isn't just about sharing knowledge—it's about sharpening your communication skills and patience. Plus, there's nothing like the joy of helping someone ace that test. Knowledge is power, and in this case, it's profitable too!

Summer & Holiday Gigs: The Cash Wave Is Calling!

Think of these gigs as your personal money-making surfboards, helping you glide over the waves of financial opportunity that roll in during these peak times.

Retail Rookies: Unleash Your Inner Sales Guru Holidays and sales go hand in hand like peanut butter and jelly. Retail stores are on the hunt for enthusiastic, go-getters like you. This is your chance to dive into the retail jungle, flex those persuasive selling muscles, and learn the art of customer service. Plus, snagging those sweet employee discounts is like the cherry on top!

Event Staffing: Be the Hero Behind the Scenes Festivals, concerts, and sports events crank up the heat during summers and holidays. And guess what? They need a crew. From ticketing to managing stalls, you're looking at fun-filled, action-packed gigs that pay. It's your backstage pass to some cool events, and you're getting paid to be there. Talk about a win-win!

Lifeguarding: Be a Baywatch Star Poolside or beachside, lifeguarding is a summer job that's both crucial and cool. It's not just about rocking those sunglasses—it's about responsibility, attentiveness, and swift action. If you've got the skills and the certification, dive into this role. Saving lives and soaking up the sun? Yes, please!

Tour Guide: Show Off Your City Know your city like the back of your hand? Why not show it off and get paid? Summer and holidays attract tourists, and they're eager to explore. Being a tour guide means sharing stories, leading adventures, and meeting people from all over the globe. Plus, you're getting paid to talk about the places you love!

Camp Counselor: Lead, Laugh, and Learn Imagine a summer filled with campfires, outdoor activities, and making kids laugh. That's the life of a camp counselor. You're part mentor, part entertainer, and all hero in the eyes of those kids. It's a chance to develop leadership skills, patience, and many fun memories.

Holiday and summer jobs are not just about padding your wallet; they're about gaining life skills, meeting new people, and creating stories you'll tell for years. Dive into these gigs with all your might. The experience you gain is just as valuable as the cash you earn.

Young Entrepreneurs: Crafting Your Own Financial Destiny

Buckle up, because we're diving into the exhilarating world of young entrepreneurship. It's more than just a fancy title—it's about being the boss of your own story, taking the reins of your financial journey, and sprinting towards success on your terms.

The Perks of Being a Young Business Whiz

Skill Set Supercharge: Entrepreneurship is more than making money—it's a full-blown skill upgrade. You'll become a pro at problem-solving, communication, and creativity. These skills are not just cool; they're life-changing and eternally valuable.

Networking: Making Connections Count. As a young entrepreneur, every person you meet is a potential door to new opportunities. You're not just collecting contacts but building a powerhouse network that can open doors throughout your career.

Mastering Money Management: Forget Monopoly—as a young business owner, you're the real deal in financial management. You'll learn the ins and outs of budgeting, investing, and saving, setting you up for a lifetime of financial savvy.

Resilience: Bouncing Back Stronger. The entrepreneurial journey is full of ups and downs, but each challenge teaches you to bounce back stronger. This resilience isn't just about business—it's a life skill that will always stand you in good stead.

Driven by Passion: What's better than earning money? Doing it with passion and purpose. As a young entrepreneur, you're not just working a job but bringing your dreams to life and living your mission daily.

Young Entrepreneurs: Cracking the Success Code

Be a Research Pro: Dive deep into your market. Understand who needs your product and what your competitors are doing. Knowledge is your best asset, so gather it and use it to your advantage.

Stay Organized: Organization is key. Keep your ideas, plans, and finances in order. A well-organized approach is crucial for smooth business operations.

Craft a Solid Business Plan: Your business plan is your roadmap. Outline your goals, strategies, and potential challenges. It's your guide through the entrepreneurial journey.

Network Effectively: Networking isn't just about meeting people—it's about building meaningful connections. Attend events, join forums, and stay active on professional platforms like LinkedIn.

Embrace Continuous Learning: The business world is always evolving. Stay informed and adaptable by continuously learning. Read, take courses, and listen to industry insights.

Take Calculated Risks: Don't shy away from risks. Evaluate them carefully and take steps that could propel your business forward. Remember, playing it too safe can sometimes be the biggest risk.

Entrepreneurs' passion, knowledge, and willingness to learn and adapt are their greatest assets. Use them well, and watch your business dreams turn into reality.

The Young Hustler's Playbook: Cool Entrepreneurial Ideas

Are you ready to turn your entrepreneurial dreams into reality but need a spark of inspiration? Well, buckle up, because I'm about to drop some fresh, fire ideas that can transform you from a daydreamer into a doer. Check out these rad entrepreneurial ventures tailor-made for the young and ambitious.

Social Media Guru: Got a knack for making viral content or building follower empires? Boom! You could be the next social media consultant or influencer. Brands are always hunting for young minds who can speak the language of the digital generation. Whether it's Instagram aesthetics or TikTok trends, your online savvy can turn into serious cheddar.

Tech Tutor: If you're a whiz at tech stuff, use that wizardry to help those still stuck in the digital Stone Age. Offer classes or one-on-one sessions, teaching skills like using smartphones, basic coding, or even setting up a killer home entertainment system. Trust me, there's a huge market of people who'd pay to get tech-savvy.

Eco-Warrior Ventures: Passionate about the planet? Start an eco-friendly biz. Think upcycling old stuff into cool new products or offering services like a mobile bicycle repair shop. It's all about that green—both for the earth and your wallet.

Personalized Arts & Crafts: Are you the artsy type? Turn that talent into a custom art business. Personalized gifts, bespoke illustrations, handcrafted jewelry—the possibilities are endless. With platforms like Etsy, you can showcase your creations to the world. Remember, in a world of mass production, handmade is the new luxury.

Health & Fitness Coach: Fitness freaks, unite! If you're all about that healthy lifestyle, why not inspire others and get paid for it? Start as a personal trainer, a yoga instructor, or even a nutrition consultant. The world's craving health gurus, and with social media, your fitness brand can go global.

Event Planner: Love organizing? Turn that into a business by planning events—birthdays, graduations, or even small community gatherings. You'll need creativity, coordination, and a knack for making things look Instagram-perfect. Start small, build a portfolio, and soon you'll be the go-to for the best parties in town.

The Multi-Lane Highway to Riches: Building Diverse Income Streams

Let's dive into the big game – building multiple streams of income. It's like playing a real-life version of Monopoly, but instead of buying properties, you're investing in different ways to make your wallet thicker. Let's break down why it's not just cool but crucial to have more than one income stream and how it can turn your financial life into a victory lap.

Stress Be Gone! Let's keep it real—relying on just one income source? That's like walking a tightrope without a safety net. Diversifying your income is like having a bunch of safety nets—if one job goes south, you have others to keep you afloat. It's about turning that financial anxiety into peace of mind. Imagine sleeping like a baby, knowing you've got several money pipes filling your bank account.

Goals? Check! Dreaming of that dope sneaker collection, a tricked-out gaming rig, or maybe a gap year traveling the world? Multiple income streams can fast-track these dreams. It's simple math—more money means you can save for that dream faster. It's like having turbo boosters on your savings plan.

No More Income Rollercoasters: Life's all about ups and downs, and so is income, especially if you're freelancing or running your gig. Having different income sources evens out the bumps. When one gig is slow, another might be booming. It's about not putting all your eggs in one basket. Diverse income streams keep the cash flow steady, so you're not freaking out when one stream hits a dry spell.

Chase That Passion: Maybe you've got a passion project that doesn't pay much (yet), or you want to volunteer for a cause you believe in. Extra income streams can give you the financial cushion to pursue what sets your soul on fire. It's about living life on your terms rather than succumbing to a life dictated by a paycheck.

Learn, Grow, and Level Up: Each income stream is a new learning experience. You'll pick up skills and knowledge along the way—from managing an online store to mastering the stock market. It's like getting paid to go to the school of life. These skills pad your resume and make you a more rounded, savvy individual.

Building That Empire: Lastly, more income streams mean more money to invest and grow. It's like playing a real-life strategy game where you're constantly leveling up your financial power. You can reinvest in your ventures, save up for bigger investments, or even start new projects. It's about building an empire, one stream at a time.

Cash Flow Showdown: Passive Income vs. Active Income: Let's crash into the world of income types—the flashy Active Income and the cool, mysterious Passive Income. Understanding these two is like learning the cheat codes in the game of wealth-building. So, buckle up—we're about to take a deep dive into what makes these income types tick and how you can harness their power to build your treasure chest.

Active Income: Hustle Hard. First up, active income. This is your bread and butter, the classic "work for money" scenario. Think 9-to-5 jobs, side hustles, or any gig where you trade time for cash. It's like being a warrior on the financial battlefield—every dollar earned directly results from your efforts.

But here's the kicker—active income has its limits. There are only so many hours in a day, which means there's a cap on how much you can earn. It's like trying to fill a bathtub with the tap on full blast, but the plug's not in. However, don't knock it just yet. Active income is often the starting line for most people on their journey to financial greatness.

Passive Income: Money While You Sleep

Now, let's talk about the cool cat of income types—passive income. This is where you earn money with minimal ongoing effort. It's not about working harder, but smarter. Imagine planting a money tree—you put in the work upfront and then sit back and watch it bear fruit over and over again.

Stock Market Wizards: Investing in the stock market can be like having a golden goose. With the right strategy, your investments can grow while you're binge-watching your favorite show. Remember, it's about playing the long game—think compound interest, the slow but sure way your money multiplies over time.

Digital Goldmines: Creating digital products—think e-books, online courses, or digital art—can be a gold mine. You create once and sell infinitely. It's like recording a hit song and earning royalties every time it's played.

Affiliate Marketing: Cash from Commissions. Got a knack for recommending products? Affiliate marketing lets you earn commission by promoting other people's products. It's like being a treasure guide, leading people to hidden gems and getting a finder's fee.

YouTube Stardom: Start a YouTube channel about something you're passionate about. Once your channel hits it big, ad revenue and sponsorships can turn into a sweet passive income stream. It's like having your own TV show, but you're the boss.

Passive vs. Active: The Tag Team. The secret to financial freedom? Don't choose one—combine both passive and active income. Use your active income to fund your passive income ventures. It's like being a financial ninja, using every weapon in your arsenal. Active income gets you in the game; passive income changes the rules.

Juggling the Hustle: Mastering the Art of Balancing Part-Time Jobs and Academics

Let's tackle the tightrope walk of balancing part-time jobs and academics. You're not just aiming to make bank—you're also gunning for those grades. It's like being a DJ mixing two tracks to create the perfect harmony. Let's dive into the strategies that'll help you keep your grades and bank account smiling.

Plan Your Time Effectively: The Ultimate Jigsaw Puzzle. First off, time management is your best friend. It's like being a wizard conjuring up the perfect schedule. Plot out your classes, work hours, study time, and yes, even your chill time. Apps like Google Calendar or Trello can be your digital wands, helping you keep track of your commitments. Remember, every minute counts, so plan like a pro.

Self-Care: Your Secret Weapon. Listen up, being busy is cool, but burning out? Not so much. Self-care isn't just bubble baths and yoga— it's about ensuring you're not running on empty. Eat right, sleep tight, and throw in some exercise. It's like tuning your engine for peak performance.

Flexible Jobs: Your Flex Pass to Balance. When job hunting, look for gigs that flex with your academic life. Think remote work, on-campus jobs, or gigs with flexible hours. It's like finding a dance partner who moves in sync with you.

Communication: Your Bridge to Understanding. Keep the lines of communication open with your bosses and professors. They're not mind-readers, so let them know your schedule and if things get too hectic. It's like being a captain steering your ship through rough waters with clear signals.

Optimize Your Study Environment: Your Personal Brain Gym. Create a study space that's all about focus. Make it a quiet corner in your room or a spot in the library—a no-distraction zone. Equip it with all your study essentials. It's like building your personal gym but for your brain.

Bonus Tips: The Extras That Add Up
- **Use tech to your advantage:** Apps for note-taking, studying, and managing finances can be lifesavers.

- **Seek academic help if needed:** Don't shy away from tutors or study groups.

- **Remember, quality over quantity:** Better to have focused study sessions than long, unproductive ones.

The 15-Minute Financial Journaling Challenge

Ready to turbo-charge your money-making journey? Grab a notebook or your favorite digital tool, 'cause it's time to dive deep into your financial psyche with a rapid-fire quiz. Think of it as your personal financial gym session—quick, intense, and super rewarding. Let's roll!

1. Have I identified the benefits of working as a teen or young adult, both in terms of immediate financial gains and long-term skill development?

2. What entrepreneurial skills or mindset shifts can I cultivate to maximize my earning potential?

3. Have I explored the concept of passive income, and do I understand its potential impact on my overall financial stability?

4. In what ways can I leverage online platforms to earn money, considering my skills and interests?

5. Am I aware of the various opportunities for earning money during the summer or through part-time jobs, and have I considered which aligns best with my goals?

6. What steps can I take to turn a hobby or passion into a potential income stream as a teen or young adult?

7. Have I considered the long-term benefits of developing multiple income streams, including both active and passive sources?

8. What entrepreneurial ventures or business ideas align with my interests, and how can I take the first steps toward pursuing them?

9. How can I balance the benefits of gaining work experience as a teen or young adult with the demands of my academic or personal life?

10. In what ways can I use my skills or knowledge to offer services online, creating an additional source of income?

11. What skills or certifications can I acquire to increase my value in the job market or as an entrepreneur?

12. Do I have a clear financial goal for the income I want to generate, and what steps can I take to achieve that goal?

13. What are the potential tax implications or considerations I should be aware of when earning money as a teen or young adult?

14. Have I explored creative ways to network and connect with potential employers, clients, or collaborators to enhance my earning opportunities?

Wrapping Up and Revving Up for the Next Chapter

As we wrap up this goldmine of a chapter, let's hit the rewind button and soak in all the money-making wisdom we've hustled through. We've navigated the dynamic world of earning potential, from part-time gigs to the thrilling universe of online entrepreneurship. You've been armed with the know-how to transform your passions into paychecks and discovered the art of balancing academics with earning moolah.

Remember, the key to unlocking your earning potential isn't just about stacking cash – it's about shaping a mindset that sees opportunities in challenges and embraces growth at every turn. We've explored the realms of passive income versus active hustling and how diversifying your income streams is like building your own financial Avengers team.

CHAPTER 3:

YOUR JOURNEY THROUGH BANKING

> *"You must gain control over your money, or the lack of it will forever control you."* — DAVE RAMSEY

Let's get real—banking isn't just for the suit-and-tie crowd. It's your financial playground, and it's about time you rocked it. Think of banks as your financial toolkit, ready to arm you with everything you need to handle your cash like a pro. Gone are the days when banking was a chore. Now, it's your ticket to financial freedom, baby!

How Do Banks Work?

Picture a bank like a massive money warehouse. You stash your cash there, and they keep it safe—simple, right? But there's more. Banks are like magicians with your money; they use it to make more money through loans and investments. And the cool part? They pay you for the privilege of using your dough through interest. It's a win-win!

What Services Do They Offer?

Checking Accounts: These are your everyday heroes. Need to buy a new game or pay for a concert ticket? Your checking account has got your back. It's like having a financial Swiss Army knife in your pocket.

Example: Jamie, a 17-year-old high school senior, opens her first checking account to manage her earnings from a part-time job. She learns to use online banking for convenience, sets up direct deposit for her paychecks, and uses her debit card for purchases, keeping track of her spending through the bank's mobile app. This independence helps Jamie budget for college application fees and save for her senior trip.

Credit Cards: Think of them as your financial lifeline, but with a twist. They're great for building credit and snagging rewards, but watch out—they're not free money. Use them wisely, or they'll bite back with interest.

Example: Alex, a 20-year-old college student, receives his first credit card with a modest credit limit. He uses it to pay for textbooks and monthly subscriptions, ensuring he pays the full monthly balance to avoid interest charges. This responsible usage boosts Alex's credit score, teaching him valuable lessons about credit utilization and the importance of timely payments.

Certificates of Deposit (CDs): A CD is a federally insured savings account with a fixed interest rate and fixed withdrawal date, known as the maturity date.

Example: Sofia, a 22-year-old recent graduate, receives a lump sum as a graduation gift. She invests in a CD for 12 months, locking in a higher interest rate than her savings account. This disciplined approach allows her money to grow risk-free, contributing to her savings for a future down payment on a car.

Safety First: CDs are considered one of the safest investment options, as they are insured up to $250,000 by the FDIC in banks or by the NCUA in credit unions.

How CDs Work

Fixed Terms: CDs come with terms ranging from a few months to several years. You agree to lock in your money for this period to earn interest.

Interest Rates: The interest rate on a CD is typically higher than that of a savings account because you're committing to leaving your deposit untouched for a set period.

Choosing the Right CD

Term Lengths: Short-term vs. long-term CDs—Consider how long you can afford to set aside your savings without access.

Interest Rates: Shop around for the best rates. Online banks often offer higher rates compared to traditional brick-and-mortar banks.

Penalties for Early Withdrawal: Be aware that withdrawing funds before the maturity date can result in penalties.

Loans: Need a cash infusion for college, a car, or starting your side hustle? Banks can hook you up. Just remember, it's borrowed money, so have a game plan to pay it back.

Savings Accounts: This is where your money can kick back and relax while growing steadily. Think of it as your money's cozy hammock, swinging to the rhythm of interest rates.

Example: Emma, a 15-year-old, opens a savings account to save money for a concert she wants to attend. By setting aside some of her allowance and birthday money, she watches her savings grow with interest. This achievement not only allows her to buy the concert ticket but also instills the value of saving for future goals.

Money Market Accounts

A money market account (MMA) is a type of savings account that typically offers higher interest rates in exchange for larger deposit amounts.

Example: Noah, an 18-year-old entrepreneur, opens a money market account to save the earnings from his online business. The higher interest rate and the ability to write checks offer him the flexibility to invest back into his business while earning interest on his balance. This strategic decision helps Noah manage his business finances effectively, preparing him for future financial ventures.

Access and Flexibility: Unlike CDs, MMAs allow for limited check writing and debit card access, making them a more flexible option for those who may need access to their funds.

Benefits of Money Market Accounts

Higher Interest Rates: MMAs often offer higher interest rates than traditional savings accounts, making them an attractive option for earning interest on your savings.

Ease of Access: The ability to write checks or use a debit card provides convenient access to your funds without the penalties associated with early CD withdrawals.

Insurance: Like savings accounts and CDs, money market accounts are insured up to $250,000 by the FDIC or NCUA, providing a safe haven for your money.

How to Choose a Money Market Account

Compare Interest Rates: Look for the best rates, but also pay attention to any minimum balance requirements.

Understand the Fees: Some MMAs may come with monthly maintenance fees or require a minimum balance to avoid fees.

Access to Funds: Consider how often you need to access your money and whether the account's withdrawal limitations align with your financial needs.

Remember, each of these services is a tool in your financial belt. Use them right, and you'll master your cash flow. Stay tuned for more insights on how to make these banking tools work for you!

Banking Buffet: Pick Your Flavor

Community Banks: These are like your friendly neighborhood Spider-Man but in banking. Community banks are all about local vibes. They know you, your mom, and probably your dog too. They're perfect for personalized service and a community feel.

Online Banks: Welcome to banking in your PJs! Online banks are the Netflix of the banking world—always there, anytime, anywhere. They ditch the physical branches for web and app-based services, offering you convenience and often lower fees.

Central Banks: The big bosses of the banking world. Think of central banks as financial Avengers, safeguarding an entire country's economy. They're not where you'd go to open an account, but they're pulling the strings behind the scenes, controlling things like interest rates and money supply.

Investment Banks: The Wall Street stars. Investment banks are where big money plays—we're talking mergers, acquisitions, and hefty financial deals. They're the go-to for corporations and governments when it comes to big money moves.

Each type of bank serves a unique role in the financial universe. Whether you're looking for a cozy community feel, digital convenience, or big-league financial plays, there's a bank out there that's your perfect financial match.

Checking vs. Savings Accounts: Your Money's Yin and Yang

Think of checking and savings accounts as the dynamic duo of your banking journey. They're like Batman and Robin—both super important, but each with their own superpowers.

Checking Accounts: The superheroes of daily transactions. Need to pay for a pizza, get cash from an ATM, or set up direct deposit for your part-time gig? Checking accounts is your go-to. They're all about easy access and flexibility. But remember, with great power comes great responsibility—these accounts usually don't earn much (if any) interest.

Savings Accounts: The guardians of your future dreams. Saving for a new phone, a college fund, or that epic road trip with friends? Savings accounts are your financial fortress. They keep your money safe and help it grow with interest, but they're not as flexible as checking accounts when it comes to withdrawals.

Choosing between a checking and savings account isn't an "either/or" scenario. It's more about using each for their strengths. A checking account for your daily financial hustle and a savings account for your future goals—that's how you play the banking game like a pro.

Mastering the Art of Checking Accounts

Checking Accounts: Your Financial Swiss Army Knife

How They Work: Imagine a checking account as your everyday financial sidekick. It's where your money lands—whether from a job, allowance or that birthday check from grandma—and waits for you to swing into action. These accounts are designed for frequent use, like withdrawing cash, paying bills, or using a debit card. Think of them as a convenient tool for managing daily money matters.

Checking Account Features: Not all heroes wear capes, and not all checking accounts are the same. Here's what to look for:

Debit Card: Your magic wand for purchases and ATM withdrawals.

Online and Mobile Banking: Manage your money on the go. Transfer funds, pay bills, or check your balance from your phone or computer.

Overdraft Protection: A safety net for those "oops" moments when you spend more than you have.

Monthly Fees and Minimum Balance Requirements: Some accounts charge fees or require you to maintain a minimum balance.

Choose wisely to avoid unnecessary charges.

Interest-Earning Option: A rare breed, but some checking accounts do offer interest on your balance.

How to Use a Checking Account: It's like the command center for your cash flow. Deposit your money, pay your bills, buy what you need, and track your spending. The key is to keep an eye on your balance to avoid overdrafts. Regularly review your account statements or use mobile banking apps to stay on top of your finances.

How to Choose a Checking Account

Your mission, should you choose to accept it, involves considering these factors:

Fees: Look for low or no monthly fees. Every dollar saved is a win.

ATM Access: Ensure there are convenient ATMs nearby to avoid fees.

Online Banking Features: Essential for managing your money in the digital age.

Customer Service: Good support can be a lifesaver when you hit a snag.

Perks and Bonuses: Some accounts offer sign-up bonuses or other perks. Keep an eye out for these financial treats.

Your checking account is more than just a place to stash your cash—it's a powerful tool for managing your financial life. Choose wisely, use it well, and you'll be mastering the money game in no time!

Navigating the World of Savings Accounts

How Savings Accounts Work: Picture a savings account as your financial garden—a place where your money grows. You plant your funds here, not for daily use, but for future financial goals, be it a new phone, college, or even a rainy day. Unlike checking accounts, savings accounts are designed to hold your money over time, often earning a bit of interest. Think of it as your money's cozy nest, slowly but surely getting plumper.

Pros and Cons of Savings Accounts

PROS

Safety and Security: Your money is protected (up to certain limits) by government insurance.

Interest Earnings: While not a get-rich-quick scheme, your savings do earn interest, helping your money grow over time.

Easy Access: Unlike some investments, you can usually get to your money without too many hoops or penalties.

Helps Build Financial Discipline: It's a great tool for learning the art of saving and delayed gratification.

CONS

Lower Interest Rates: Compared to other investment options, savings accounts typically offer lower returns.

Monthly Limits on Withdrawals: There's often a cap on how often you can take money out without fees or penalties.

Minimum Balance Requirements: Some accounts require you to keep a minimum amount to avoid fees or to earn interest.

Different Types of Savings Accounts

Regular Savings Accounts: The basic model—simple, straightforward, and a good starting point for new savers.

High-Yield Savings Accounts: Offers higher interest rates but might come with more conditions or limited access.

Money Market Accounts (MMAs): A savings and checking account blend. Higher interest rates usually require higher balances.

Certificates of Deposit (CDs): Consider these time-locked savings. You commit your money for a specific period (say, six months to five years) and usually get a higher interest rate. The catch? You can't touch the money without a penalty until the time's up.

Specialty Savings Accounts: Tailored for specific educational goals (Education Savings Accounts) or retirement (Individual Retirement Accounts).

The Savvy Guide to Choosing the Right Bank

When picking a bank, it's like choosing a new smartphone—you want something that fits your lifestyle, is reliable, and doesn't cost an arm and a leg. Here's your go-to guide to finding a banking partner that's just right for you.

Mobile Online Banking – Your Financial World in Your Pocket
Why It's a Big Deal: In the age of TikTok and Instagram, who wants to visit a bank physically? Mobile banking is your financial control center, available 24/7. Make sure your bank offers a user-friendly mobile app.

What to Look For: Easy transfers, mobile check deposits, real-time notifications, and robust security features.

Online Transaction Capabilities – The Power of Clicks and Taps
Digital is the Way: Ensure your bank offers comprehensive online transaction options. The ability to pay bills, transfer funds, and manage accounts online is non-negotiable.

Check for Extras: Some banks go the extra mile with features like budgeting tools or savings goals.

Banking Insurance – Your Safety Net
What it Means: Federally insured banks protect your money up to certain limits. It's like having a financial guardian angel.

Look for: FDIC insurance for traditional banks or NCUA insurance for credit unions. This insurance means your money is safe even if the bank faces trouble.

Reputation Matters – Choose a Bank That Has Good Street

Cred:

Check the Street Cred: A bank's reputation can be a deal-maker or breaker. Look for banks known for customer satisfaction, reliability, and good service.

Dig a Little Deeper: Read reviews, check ratings, and ask friends or family for their experiences.

Your Expectations - The Bank That Meets Your Wishlist

List It: Make a list of what you expect from your bank. Are you looking for low fees, high interest rates on savings, or excellent customer service?

Matchmaking: Compare your list with what different banks offer and see which one ticks the most boxes.

Fees - Because No One Likes Unpleasant Surprises

The Fee Factor: Look for a bank that charges low or no fees. This includes monthly maintenance fees, ATM fees, and overdraft charges.

Read the Fine Print: Sometimes fees are hidden in the lengthy terms and conditions. Don't hesitate to ask for clarification.

Branch and ATM Accessibility - For Those Times You Need Physical Cash

Location, Location, Location: Consider how close the bank's branches and ATMs are to your home, work, or school.

ATM Network: Ensure the bank has a wide ATM network, and check if they offer fee rebates for using other banks' ATMs.

Customer Service – Your Go-To for Help and Guidance

Why it's Key: Excellent customer service can make your banking experience smooth and stress-free.

Test the Waters: Call the customer service line before you commit. Are they helpful, knowledgeable, and easy to reach?

Interest Rates – Your Money Should Grow While It Rests

The Growth Factor: Compare interest rates for savings accounts and CDs. A higher rate means more money in your pocket.

Rate Fluctuations: Remember, interest rates can change, so consider the bank's history and stability.

Additional Services – Because Sometimes You Need More

Beyond Basics: Some banks offer additional services like wealth management, financial planning, or loan options.

Your Future Needs: Think about what you might need down the line and whether the bank can provide those services.

Technology and Innovation – Staying Ahead of the Curve

Tech-Savvy Banking: With technology evolving rapidly, choose a bank that keeps up. This includes innovations like contactless payments, advanced security measures, and AI-driven customer support.

The Cool Factor: Sometimes, it's about the cool tech features that make banking fun and easy.

User Experience – Banking Shouldn't Be a Chore

Ease of Use: Your banking experience should be intuitive, not confusing. The user interface of online and mobile platforms should be straightforward to navigate.

Seamless Experience: Transitions between different banking services (like checking to savings or mobile to desktop) should be seamless.

Choosing a bank is like picking a partner for a financial marathon. It's about finding a good match for your needs, aspirations, and lifestyle. Take your time, do your homework, and remember, you're in the driver's seat. A great banking experience can pave the way for a smooth financial journey, so choose wisely and bank smartly!

The Balancing Act: Pros and Cons of Online Banking

In the rapidly evolving world of finance, online banking has become a cornerstone for personal money management. But like any innovation, it comes with its advantages and drawbacks. Let's weigh the pros and cons to help you make informed decisions about integrating online banking into your financial life.

The Upside of Online Banking
PROS

Speed and Efficiency: Online banking is a game-changer in terms of efficiency. Transactions that once required a trip to the bank now happen instantaneously. Whether it's transferring funds, paying bills, or checking account balances, online banking executes these tasks with remarkable speed.

Unmatched Convenience: The convenience offered by online banking is unparalleled. Accessibility around the clock from any location with internet access means your bank is always open. This flexibility is particularly beneficial for those with busy schedules or living in areas with limited banking services.

The Flip Side: Considering the Cons
CONS

Security Concerns: While banks invest heavily in cybersecurity, online banking is not immune to risks. Phishing scams, identity theft, and data breaches are real threats. Users must be vigilant, using strong, unique passwords, and be cautious about the networks they use for banking.

Lack of Personal Interaction: Some banking matters benefit from face-to-face interaction. Complex issues like loan applications or financial planning can be challenging to navigate online. For those who value personal connection and advice, the impersonal nature of online banking can be a downside.

Safeguarding Your Digital Vault: Secure Online Banking Practices

In the age of digital banking, safeguarding your financial information is as crucial as locking your physical wallet. Let's dive into some ironclad strategies to keep your money and personal data secure while you navigate the convenience of online banking.

Regular Password Updates: The First Line of Defense

Stay One Step Ahead: Regularly changing your online banking passwords is akin to frequently changing the locks on your doors. It helps prevent unauthorized access, even if your password has been compromised.

Fortifying Your Passwords

Complexity is Key: A strong password acts as a formidable gatekeeper. Think of it as a complex combination lock. Combine letters, numbers, and special characters in unexpected ways to create passwords that are difficult for hackers to guess.

Diligent Account Monitoring: Your Vigilant Eye

Routine Checks: Frequently reviewing your bank statements and account activity is akin to a regular health check-up for your finances. It helps in early detection of any unauthorized transactions or suspicious activities.

Avoid Public Wi-Fi for Banking Transactions

Public vs. Private: Conducting banking transactions over public Wi-Fi is like having a confidential conversation in a crowded room. Always use a secure, private connection to keep your financial data confidential.

The Added Shield of Multifactor Authentication

Double Locking Your Digital Door: Multifactor authentication adds an extra layer of security. It's like having a double lock system where gaining access requires more than just the key (your password), ensuring your account remains secure even if one credential is compromised.

The Power of Banking Apps

In today's fast-paced world, banking apps are like having a financial Swiss Army knife in your pocket—versatile, convenient, and indispensable. Let's explore why these apps are revolutionizing how we handle money and some top recommendations for your banking needs.

Benefits of Using Banking Apps

Instant Access: Banking apps put financial control in your hands, anytime, anywhere. It's like having a mini bank branch in your pocket.

Real-Time Notifications: Stay informed with instant alerts on transactions and account changes, like a personal finance watchdog.

Effortless Money Management: Track spending, set budgets, and analyze financial trends—all in one place. It's like having a financial advisor at your beck and call.

Quick Transactions: Transfer funds, pay bills, or deposit checks with just a few taps. Think of it as your financial express lane.

Top Banking Apps for Teens and Young Adults

Greenlight: Ideal for teens learning money management, Greenlight offers parental controls, spending tracking, and saving goals.

Step: Tailored for young adults, Step combines banking with financial education. It's like a financial toolkit designed for the digital age.

Chime: Great for those who want a simplified banking experience with no hidden fees. It's like having a straightforward, no-nonsense financial ally.

Launching Your Banking Journey: Opening Your First Account

Embarking on your financial journey begins with a significant first step—opening your first bank account. This is your gateway to financial independence and savvy money management. Whether you're a teen or a young adult, this guide will walk you through the process, ensuring it's a breeze. And for the younger folks, having a parent or guardian by your side can be a great support. Let's get started.

Ready to start your banking journey? Here's a step-by-step guide to opening your first account. Check it off as you go, and welcome to the world of smart banking.

Step-by-Step Guide to Opening Your First Bank Account

Choose Your Bank Wisely: Reflect on the insights from this chapter. Consider factors like online banking features, account fees, and bank reputation.

Select the Right Account Type: Decide between a checking or savings account based on your financial goals. For teens, a joint account with parents is often a good start.

Gather Necessary Documents: You'll need identification (like a passport or driver's license), proof of address, and sometimes a minimum deposit.

Visit the Bank or Apply Online: Many banks offer the convenience of online applications. For a more personal touch, visit a local branch.

Fill Out the Application: Whether online or in-person, fill out the application form with your details. Double-check for accuracy to avoid any hiccups.

Submit and Wait for Approval: The bank will review your application once submitted. This process is usually quick, especially for straightforward accounts.

Deposit Funds: After approval, make your initial deposit to activate the account. This can often be done electronically or in person.

Set Up Online Banking: If available, set up your online banking to start managing your account digitally.

Explore Banking Features: Familiarize yourself with your new account's features—like mobile banking apps or savings tools.

If you're a teen, involve your parents in this process. Their experience and guidance can be invaluable, and some banks require a parent for minors to open an account. This is more than just a formality—it's a shared step towards your financial growth.

Segue: Wrapping Up Your Banking Odyssey

You've just navigated through the dynamic world of banking like a pro. Remember, understanding banking isn't just about numbers and accounts; it's about unlocking doors to your financial freedom. You've got the lowdown on everything from the nitty-gritty of different bank accounts to the digital magic of online banking. You're not just ready to make savvy banking choices—you're set to transform them into power moves for your financial future.

Key Takeaways

Banking Know-How: You've unraveled the mysteries of how banks work, diving deep into their services, from checking to savings and beyond.

Digital Banking Mastery: Online banking is your new playground. You've learned to navigate it with ease, prioritizing security and convenience.

First Account Milestone: Armed with the knowledge to choose your first bank account wisely, you're confidently stepping into the banking world.

What's Next? Hold onto Your Hats!

As we close this chapter, prepare to turn the page to an even more exhilarating journey. Up next, we're tackling the world of credit and loans. Think of it as the sequel where you become the hero of your credit story.

Credit Unveiled: We'll debunk myths, lay out the facts, and give you the tools to build and maintain stellar credit.

Loan Landscape: From student loans to mortgages, we'll explore how to navigate loans responsibly, turning them from daunting debts to strategic tools.

You're building a foundation that's not just about surviving the financial tide but thriving in it. So, gear up for the next chapter, where you'll continue to grow from a savvy saver to a credit connoisseur. Your financial empowerment saga continues, and trust me, it's about to get even more exciting!

CHAPTER 4:

BUDGETING MASTERY

"You must gain control over your money, or the lack of it will forever control you." — DAVE RAMSEY

Picture this: You're at the helm of a ship, navigating through the wild seas of finance. Sounds dramatic? Well, managing your money without a budget is like sailing without a compass—clueless and risky. Dave Ramsey hit the nail on the head when he said, "You must gain control over your money or the lack of it will forever control you." That's what this chapter is about—seizing the reins, steering clear of financial shipwrecks, and charting a course to treasure islands filled with financial freedom and stability.

Budgeting Explained

So, what's budgeting anyway? Strip away the financial jargon, and it's about knowing what's coming in, what's going out, and what's staying put. It's your financial blueprint, your game plan. Think of it as the financial fitness plan for your wallet—tailored to flex those savings muscles while trimming the fat off your expenses.

What Budgeting Is Not: First off, let's debunk a myth. Budgeting isn't about skimping on lattes or never seeing the inside of a movie theater again. It's not a financial straightjacket meant to squeeze the fun out of life. Nah, it's quite the opposite. Budgeting is about making your money work for you, not about you slaving away for your money.

The Ingredients of a Solid Budget: At its core, a budget has a few key components:

- **Income:** This is your firepower, your ammo. It's every penny that comes your way, be it from a job, side hustles, or the Bank of Mom and Dad.

- **Expenses:** These are the waves trying to capsize your financial ship—needs, wants, and the sneaky "I just gotta haves."

- **Savings & Goals:** The treasure chest. This is where you stash the loot for future adventures—be it college, a car, or that concert you can't miss.

Why Budget? If you're thinking, "Why should I bother?" let me lay it out for you. Budgeting is about freedom—the freedom to live your life on your terms, knowing your financial ship is sturdy, leaks are patched, and you're on course to your dream destinations.

Making It Personal: The beauty of budgeting? It's all you. Custom-tailored to fit your life, your dreams, and your goals. Whether you're saving up for a gaming console, plotting your escape to college, or simply trying to avoid the broke teen trope, your budget is the map to get you there.

The Importance of Budgeting

Talking about budgeting often gets the same reaction as mentioning a visit to the dentist—necessary but not exactly fun. But here's the kicker: Mastering the art of budgeting is like unlocking a cheat code for life. It's not about pinching pennies until they scream; it's about making your money scream your name from the rooftops, celebrating your financial savvy.

Live Like a King in Retirement: Imagine sipping a cool drink on a beach in your golden years, not a care in the world. Sounds dreamy, right? That's the power of a budget that works for you, not against you. Budgeting isn't about depriving yourself today—it's about ensuring you're living it up tomorrow. It's about stashing that cash so you can retire not just comfortably, but like royalty.

The Emergency Life Raft: Life loves to throw curveballs—car repairs, unexpected medical bills, or that surprise concert you just can't miss. Without a budget, these surprises can sink you faster than a lead balloon. With a budget, you've got an emergency raft ready to go. It's about being prepared, so when life does its thing, you're saying, "Bring it on," instead of, "Oh no."

The Debt-Free Dance: Ever felt the weight of debt on your shoulders? It's like carrying a backpack full of bricks—every step is harder. Budgeting is your personal debt demolition team. It's about knowing your limits so you don't spend money that isn't yours to begin with. And when you're living debt-free, every step feels like a dance.

Goals and Dreams: The Blueprint. What's on your bucket list? A world tour, your startup, or maybe a sleek, new ride? A budget is your blueprint to turn those dreams into reality. It's about setting your sights on the prize and charting a course to get there. Without a budget, goals are just wishes. With it, they're a work in progress.

Kicking Bad Habits to the Curb: We've all got them—those little spending habits that add up to big money drains. That daily gourmet coffee, impulse online shopping, or the "treat yo'self" mentality that treats your wallet like a punching bag. Budgeting shines a spotlight on these habits, helping you kick them to the curb. It's not about never indulging; it's about indulging smartly and with purpose.

What to Include in Your Budget: Teen Edition

Alright, young moguls, let's talk about crafting that budget—a blueprint for your financial empire. You've heard it all before, from "track your spending," to "save for a rainy day," but what does that look like when you're more worried about prom than pensions? Let's break it down and focus on what's going to your budget as epic as your dreams.

The Essentials: Keepin' You Running. First up, we've got the essentials. This isn't just about food and a roof over your head (though those are pretty important). We're talking phone bills, internet (because, let's face it, no one's surviving without WiFi), and transportation. Whether it's gas money or that bus pass, getting from A to B without breaking the bank is key.

The Future Fund: Your Dreams Aren't Free. Next, we're stashing cash for the future. Call it your "Dream Fund." Whether you're saving up for college, a car, or to start your own business, this is where you put a piece of your pie away for the big-ticket items that'll get you where you want to go. Think of it as investing in your future self.

The Fun Factor: All Work and No Play? Nah. You're only young once, right? A solid budget includes some fun money. Whether it's concerts, movies, or just hanging out with friends, make sure you've got a line in your budget for fun. It's about balance, finding joy in the now while building for tomorrow.

The Oops Fund: Because Life Happens. Unexpected expenses? Welcome to life. That's why you need an "Oops Fund." This is your financial safety net for when your phone decides to take a swim, or your laptop goes on the fritz right before finals. It's not *if* life throws you a curveball—it's ***when***.

The Giving Back Line: Good Vibes Only. Last but not least, budget a little for giving back. Whether it's donating to a cause you care about or buying your friend a birthday gift, having a bit set aside for others can make a big difference, not just in their lives, but in how you feel about your money story.

Guide to Budget Mastery

Imagine you're building your dream gaming PC. You wouldn't just go out and buy random parts, right? You'd need a plan: What components you need, how much you're willing to spend, and what performance you expect. That's what budgeting is in the financial world—your blueprint for building the life you want without running out of cash.

Step 1: Calculate Your Net Income: The first step in crafting your budget is figuring out how much money you actually have to work with. For you, this might mean tallying up your allowance, part-time job earnings, birthday money, and any other income. Remember, net income is what you have after taxes are taken out, so make sure you're working with the right numbers.

Step 2: Track Your Spending: Next, act like a detective on your own financial case. Keep track of every dollar spent for a month—whether it's on games, clothes, snacks, or savings. You might use an app, a spreadsheet, or old-school pen and paper. The goal is to see where your money is going, especially those sneaky, unnoticed expenses that add up.

Step 3: Set Realistic Goals: Now, dream a bit. What do you want your money to do for you? Maybe it's saving for a new laptop, affording a concert ticket, or having an emergency fund. Your goals should be SMART: Specific, Measurable, Achievable, Relevant, and Time-bound. A goal like "Save $200 for a concert in six months" checks all these boxes.

Step 4: Make a Plan: Armed with knowledge of your income, spending, and goals, start drafting your budget. Allocate funds for your needs first (like savings and essentials), then for your wants (like entertainment). There are various budgeting methods—like the 50/30/20 rule (needs/wants/savings)—but choose what best fits your lifestyle and goals.

Step 5: Adjust Your Spending to Stay on Budget: This is where the rubber meets the road. If you're overspending in one area, you'll need to cut back somewhere else. Maybe that means fewer lattes to keep your gaming fund intact. It's all about making trade-offs that align with your priorities.

Step 6: Review Your Budget Regularly: Your budget isn't set in stone. Life changes, and so will your financial situation and goals. Make it a habit to review and adjust your budget regularly—say, every month or whenever a major financial change occurs. This keeps you on track and in control of your financial journey.

How to Stick to Your Budget Like a Pro

Locking down a budget is step one. Sticking to it? That's where the real game begins. Here's how you can stay on track without feeling like you're on a financial leash. It's about being smart, not scarce.

Sleep on Big Purchases: Ever felt the rush of impulse buying only to face buyer's remorse the next day? Here's a pro tip: Hit pause. Give yourself a 24-hour timeout before making any large purchases. It's not about saying no—it's about saying, "Let me sleep on it." You'd be surprised how often the thrill fades by morning.

Never Spend More Than You Have: Sounds like a no-brainer, right? But in the age of credit cards and buy-now-pay-later schemes, it's easier than ever to spend money you don't actually have. Live by this mantra: If it's not in your bank, it's not in your budget.

Stick to a Lower Credit Card Limit: Speaking of credit cards, they're not the enemy—but they do need to be tamed. A lower credit limit isn't just about reducing temptation; it's a safety net that keeps your potential debt in check. Plus, it's a sweet relief not to have a maxed-out card hanging over your head.

Budget to Zero: Every dollar needs a job. By assigning every penny to a category (yes, including savings and fun money), you give every bit of your income a purpose. This way, you know exactly where your money's going, and you get to see the real power of your paycheck.

Try a No-Spend Challenge: Ready to level up? Take on a no-spend challenge. Whether it's for a weekend or a whole month, challenge yourself to spend nothing beyond the essentials. It's not just about saving money; it's about discovering what you can live without and what truly adds value to your life.

Stop Paying for Fees: Late fees, ATM fees, subscription fees—they add up faster than you can say "budget buster." Get vigilant. Automate bill payments, use your bank's ATM, and regularly review subscriptions. If you're not using it, lose it.

Plan Your Meals: Eating out is a budget's kryptonite. Start meal planning and cooking at home to save some serious dough. Not only will your wallet thank you, but you might just unleash your inner chef.

Do Your Grocery Shopping Online: Impulse buys are harder to resist when you're wandering the aisles. Switch to online grocery shopping to stick to your list and avoid those sneaky extras that jump into your cart when you're not looking.

Teen-Friendly Budgeting Methods

Navigating the financial world as a teen can be like entering a maze without a map. However, mastering the art of budgeting early on can turn you into a financial wizard, capable of making your money work for you, not against you. Here's a quick overview of some top budgeting methods tailored for teens, each designed to fit different spending habits and financial goals.

The 50/30/20 Rule Explained

Imagine your finances as a pie chart (and who doesn't love pie?). The 50/30/20 rule slices this pie into three essential parts: needs, wants, and savings. Here's the breakdown:

50% on Needs: These are your must-haves, the essentials. Think rent (if you're out on your own), groceries, and transportation.

30% on Wants: This slice is for the fun stuff. Movie nights, that latest video game, or a trendy pair of sneakers fall into this category.

20% on Savings: The final slice is for your future. It's about building a safety net and funding your dreams, whether that's college, a car, or a trip abroad.

The 50/30/20 rule isn't just about splitting your cash—it's a strategic approach to managing your finances. It ensures you're covering essentials, enjoying life, and saving for the future, all while living within your means.

Pay-Yourself-First Budgeting: Emphasize saving before any spending. By allocating funds to your savings as soon as you receive money, you prioritize your future financial well-being, ensuring you build wealth and security.

Zero-based budgeting: Make every dollar count by assigning each to specific expenses, savings, or investments, ensuring meticulous financial management and accountability. It requires detailed tracking and planning, ensuring every penny is purposefully spent or saved.

Envelope Budgeting: Use this tactile method of managing finances by dividing cash into envelopes for different spending categories. It curbs impulse spending by making you physically see and feel your spending limits, promoting disciplined money management and financial awareness.

Budgeting tools and apps

Managing finances wisely is crucial for teens in the digital era, where budgeting apps simplify financial management beyond traditional spreadsheets. These tools offer real-time tracking, spending insights, and educational resources to empower teens with financial knowledge.

YNAB (You Need A Budget): Acts as a digital financial mentor, applying the envelope system to modern budgeting, pushing users to allocate every dollar wisely and offering educational resources for financial literacy.

Mint: Serves as a comprehensive financial overview, automating expense tracking, categorization, and budgeting alerts, simplifying the journey toward financial goals.

PocketGuard: Safeguards against overspending by monitoring accounts, highlighting recurring expenses, and calculating available spending money, aiding in smarter financial decisions.

Goodbudget: Digitizes the envelope budgeting method for easy spending allocation across categories, ideal for visual learners and family budgeting with its device-sharing capabilities.

Gohenry: Introduces teens to money management through a customizable debit card, offering lessons on earning, saving, and spending, supported by tasks and goals to instill financial discipline.

With a variety of features tailored to individual needs and learning styles, these apps make budgeting accessible and engaging for teens, encouraging a proactive approach to financial management.

Overcoming Budget Guilt

Overcoming budget guilt isn't just about cutting out unnecessary expenses; it's about reshaping your relationship with money and understanding that everyone makes financial missteps. Here's how to turn guilt into growth:

Acknowledge Your Feelings: Recognize that feeling guilty about spending is a sign you want to improve your financial habits. This acknowledgment is the first step toward making positive changes.

Reevaluate Your Budget

Assess your spending patterns: Look at where your money is going. Are there areas where you're overspending without realizing it?

Align spending with values: Ensure your budget reflects what's truly important to you, whether that's saving for the future, investing in experiences, or supporting causes you care about.

Learn from Past Mistakes

Identify triggers: What prompts you to make decisions you later regret? Recognizing these can help you avoid similar situations in the future.

Adjust your budget accordingly: Use your insights to tweak your budget, perhaps allocating funds differently or setting aside a specific amount for "guilt-free" spending.

Set Achievable Goals

Short-term wins: Create small, manageable financial goals to build confidence and a sense of accomplishment.

Celebrate responsibly: When you reach a goal, celebrate in a way that doesn't undermine your financial progress.

Practice Forgiveness and Patience:
Be kind to yourself: Understand that mastering money management is a journey. Forgive past missteps and focus on moving forward.

Stay the course: Consistency and patience are key. Your financial habits will improve over time with continued effort and mindfulness.

By adopting these strategies, you can transform feelings of guilt into empowering motivations that drive smarter financial decisions, ultimately leading to a healthier, guilt-free relationship with money.

They Did It, And So Can You!

Imagine the story of Maya, a college sophomore who found herself drowning in debt from student loans and credit card expenses. Determined to turn her financial situation around, Maya adopted the 50/30/20 budgeting rule. She meticulously allocated 50% of her income to essentials, 30% to wants, and 20% to savings and debt repayment. Within a year, Maya not only reduced her credit card debt by half but also started a savings fund.

Then there's Alex, a recent high school graduate with a passion for gaming. Alex decided to channel his passion into a side hustle by streaming his gameplay. By using the "Pay Yourself First" budgeting method, he ensured a portion of every paycheck went straight into his savings account, even before covering his monthly expenses. Alex's discipline helped him save enough to invest in better streaming equipment, boosting his online presence and income.

These stories underscore a vital lesson: Mastering budgeting is achievable with determination and the right strategy. Maya and Alex are just two examples of young individuals who took control of their finances, paving their way to financial stability. Their journeys illustrate that regardless of your starting point, with perseverance and the right budgeting method, financial mastery is within reach.

The 15-Minute Budgeting Blitz: Your Quick-Start Guide to Financial Freedom

Let's cut to the chase: Budgeting sounds like a chore, right? But what if I told you that in just 15 minutes, you could start taking control of your cash flow, just like a boss managing a Fortune 500 company? This isn't your grandma's budgeting advice. We're talking about a fast, furious, and fun way to get your finances in shape without missing a beat on your social life or your dreams.

Step 1: The Quick Setup (3 Minutes): Grab your weapon of choice: a notepad, a budgeting app, or a simple spreadsheet. Title it "My 15-Minute Money Mastery."

Step 2: Income Snapshot (2 Minutes): Jot down your monthly take-home pay. If it varies, average it out based on the past three months. We're keeping it real—no guesswork, just hard numbers.

Step 3: Speedy Spending Summary (5 Minutes): List your non-negotiables: rent, phone bill, transportation, and yes, that streaming service subscription (we're realistic, not stingy). Then, estimate your usual spending on groceries, eating out, and other essentials. Keep it lean—we're on the clock.

Step 4: Quick Save and Splurge Allocation (3 Minutes): Here's where the 50/30/20 rule kicks in. Of what's left, aim to save 20%, keep 30% for those "just because" moments, and use 50% for the fixed and variable essentials you listed. Adjust as needed, but remember—discipline is key.

Step 5: The 15-Second Reality Check (2 Minutes): Look at your plan. Is it realistic? If your coffee habit is eating into your savings, consider brewing at home. The goal is to find balance without feeling like you're in a financial lockdown.

Why This Rocks

• **It's Fast:** You've got things to do, places to be. This routine gets your finances sorted in less time than it takes to watch a YouTube tutorial on "How to Make Avocado Toast."

• **It's Flexible:** Got a side hustle or a sudden expense? Adjust your budget on the fly. This isn't set in stone; it's more like a Snapchat story – it can change as you do.

- **It's Fun:** Okay, maybe not as fun as a midnight fast-food run with friends, but seeing your savings grow and your debt shrink? That's pretty darn satisfying.

This 15-minute routine is your first step towards that. It's not about cutting corners; it's about enhancing your financial IQ, one quick session at a time. And remember, the best time to start was yesterday. The next best time? Right now.

Segue

And there you have it—the blueprint to your financial game plan is all set with budgeting skills that could rival any financial guru's strategy. You've got the tools, the techniques, and the tech to make your money work for you, not against you. We've busted the myth that budgeting is a bore and turned it into your secret weapon for financial freedom.

But hold up, we're not hitting the brakes yet. Next up, we're shifting gears into the realm of saving and investing. Imagine turning your budget surplus into a growing wealth mountain. Sounds epic, right? That's because it is. So, buckle up because we're about to take a deep dive into making your money multiply. Ready to explore how savvy saving and intelligent investing can supercharge your financial future? Let's roll into the next chapter with our eyes on the prize: building wealth that lasts.

CHAPTER 5:

SAVING FOR A RAINY DAY

"*Predicting rain doesn't count. Building arks does.*" This gem from Warren Buffett isn't just about weather forecasts—it's a life lesson in preparation and action. Think about it: Anyone can talk about what's coming, but only the wise and the brave start building their arks. So, as we dive into this chapter, remember, we're not just saving for a rainy day—we're constructing our financial arks.

Saving vs Investing – What Comes First?

In money mastery, the big question often is: Should I save or should I invest? It's like asking, "Do I buy the hammer or the nail first?" You kind of need both to build something solid. But let's break it down, Robert Kiyosaki style.

First off, saving is your financial safety net. It's the cash you stash and don't touch unless it's a "code red" situation. This is your "just in case" fund—just in case the car breaks down, just in case you need to fly to

Timbuktu, or just in case you find the perfect limited-edition sneakers (okay, maybe not the sneakers).

Investing, on the other hand, is how you grow your stash. It's putting your money into ventures that could bring back more money. It's like planting seeds and watching them grow into a garden of cash trees.

So, what comes first? In the playbook of financial freedom, saving is your defense, and investing is your offense. You got to protect what you've got before you go scoring more points. Aim to save a solid emergency fund first—think 3 to 6 months of living expenses. Once you've got that cushion, start channeling your inner investor and put your money to work. Remember, the goal isn't just to save money but to use it as a tool to build wealth and security. Like Buffett building his ark, we're not just waiting for the storm to pass—we're preparing to sail through it with confidence.

Reasons to save money

In a world awash with temptations to spend and splurge, saving money might feel like an uphill battle, especially for teens navigating their financial independence. Yet, understanding the importance of saving is crucial, not just as a buffer against unforeseen events but as a strategic move towards a prosperous future. Saving isn't about depriving yourself of fun and enjoyment—it's about empowering your future self with financial security and opportunities.

Long-term Security: Saving money lays the foundation for a life with fewer financial worries. It allows you to make important life choices, like buying a car or securing a college education, without financial constraints.

Financial Independence: Every dollar saved brings you closer to financial independence. Savings give you the freedom to make choices about your life and future, whether it's funding your education, starting a business, or traveling the world.

Taking Calculated Risks: A financial safety net enables you to take calculated risks, like starting a side hustle or investing in a venture, without jeopardizing your basic needs or plunging into debt.

Reducing Stress: Having savings reduces stress and anxiety about finances, allowing you to focus more on studies, hobbies, and personal growth.

Benefiting from Compound Interest: Starting to save early lets you take advantage of compound interest, where your savings earn interest, and that interest earns interest. Even small amounts saved regularly can grow into substantial sums over time.

The Early Bird Gets the Financial Freedom

Starting to save early isn't just about accumulating a pile of cash—it's about building a fortress of financial freedom and security. Here's how embarking on this journey now sets you up for a future where financial constraints don't dictate your life choices:

Better Retirement: Imagine a retirement where you're not just surviving but thriving. Saving from your teenage years can turn this into reality, allowing you to enjoy your golden years without financial worries. The earlier you start, the more you benefit from compound interest, turning even small savings into significant sums.

Financial Security: Starting early means you're less likely to be caught off guard by life's inevitable curveballs. It means having the backup to support you through college, a career change, or any of life's transitions without the panic that comes from living paycheck to paycheck.

Investment Opportunities: With a robust savings account, you're in a prime position to invest. Whether it's stocks, bonds, or real estate, having the capital to invest can exponentially increase your wealth, opening doors to financial growth that spending could never achieve.

Limits Debt: The temptation to rely on credit cards or loans diminishes significantly when you have your own savings to fall back on. This proactive approach to saving discourages debt accumulation, keeping your financial slate clean and your stress levels low.

Emergencies: Life is unpredictable—the car breaks down, the laptop gives up the ghost right before finals. An emergency fund ensures that these hiccups don't derail your financial stability or your future plans.

Learning about Financial Goals: Saving teaches you about setting and achieving goals. Whether it's saving for a new phone, a car, or college tuition, the discipline and planning involved lay the groundwork for bigger life goals and dreams.

Reduced Tax Liability: Understanding how to save efficiently, including taking advantage of tax-advantaged savings accounts, can reduce your tax burden, leaving more money in your pocket to grow and invest.

Ability to Pursue Opportunities: Ever dreamed of backpacking through Europe, starting your own business, or taking a gap year to volunteer? Savings give you the freedom to chase these dreams without financial constraints, turning "I wish I could" into "I'm glad I did."

Financial Control: Starting to save early puts you in the driver's seat of your financial journey. It's about taking control, making informed decisions, and steering your life in the direction of your choosing, not being at the mercy of circumstances.

Short-term vs. long-term saving goals

Navigating the seas of financial planning, the distinction between short-term and long-term saving goals stands as a beacon, guiding your journey toward financial stability and success. It's crucial to steer your savings ship with a keen eye on both the immediate shores and the distant horizon. Here's how to chart your course:

Short-term Saving Goals: Your Immediate Treasures
Short-term goals are the islands close to shore, reachable within a year or

two. These might include saving for a concert ticket, a new gadget, or a mini-vacation. The key here is specificity and immediacy. To achieve these goals, you'll need to:

Set Clear Targets: Know exactly what you're saving for and how much you need.

Short-term Strategies: Consider a separate savings account or a money jar for visual motivation. Automate your savings if possible, diverting a small portion of your allowance or income directly towards these goals.

Long-term Saving Goals: Charting Distant Lands. Long-term goals are your continents on the far horizon, requiring years of navigation. These encompass saving for college tuition, a car, or even your first home. Attaining these milestones requires a more disciplined approach:

Vision and Patience: Understand that these goals are marathons, not sprints. The discipline you build through short-term saving will be invaluable here.

Growth-focused Strategies: Look into high-interest savings accounts, certificates of deposit, or even basic investing options suitable for your age and risk tolerance. The goal is not just to save but to grow your money over time.

Practical saving strategies

A saving journey isn't just about stashing away cash—it's also about building a future as bright and bold as your dreams. And let me tell you, it's never too early or too late to start. Here are some rock-solid strategies to fuel your saving saga, perfect for the teen ready to take on the world:

Saving With a Purpose: First off, saving isn't a chore—it's your ticket to freedom and independence. Every dollar saved today is a step toward that concert, college fund, or even your first car. Define what you're saving for—be as vivid as possible. Visualizing your goals makes them real and reachable.

Set a Savings Goal: Goals are the GPS for your saving journey. Without them, you're just wandering. Break down your dreams into achievable targets. Want a new bike by summer? Figure out how much you need and when. This gives your saving purpose and a timeline.

Work Out a Percentage: Diving your income into saving and spending portions keeps you disciplined. A golden rule? Save at least 20% of what you earn or receive. It's about finding that sweet spot where you're saving effectively without feeling like you're missing out.

Make a "Fun Money" Budget: All work and no play? No way. Allocate a portion of your money for pure enjoyment. This "fun money" is your guilt-free spending zone. It ensures you enjoy life now while building for the future.

Track Their Spending: You can't manage what you don't measure. Keep an eye on where your money's is going with a spending diary or an app. It's an eye-opener to see how small purchases add up over time.

Think Twice Before Spending: Impulse buys are the arch-nemesis of saving. Before you splurge, ask yourself, "Do I really need this?" Often, waiting 24 hours before making a purchase can save you from buyer's remorse and save your wallet.

Help Job Hunt: Earning your own money is empowering and educational. Whether it's a part-time gig, freelancing, or odd jobs for neighbors, earning gives you a sense of responsibility and a bigger budget to manage.

Shop Second-Hand: There's treasure in thrift stores, online marketplaces, and garage sales. Buying second-hand not only saves you a bundle but also supports sustainability. It's a win-win.

Embrace Financial Education: Knowledge is power, especially when it comes to money. Dive into books, blogs, and courses on personal finance. The more you know, the smarter you'll save and spend.

Automate Your Savings: Make saving as effortless as breathing. Set up automatic transfers to your savings account. It's like playing a financial game where you set the rules and score with every deposit.

Celebrate Milestones: Reward yourself for hitting savings milestones. It could be a movie night, a small purchase, or an outing with friends. Celebrating victories keeps motivation high and the saving journey fun.

Make saving money a habit

Transforming saving into a habit is about empowering yourself to live your dream life. It takes practice, patience, and savvy. Here's how to make saving as natural as scrolling through your social feeds.

Pay Yourself First: The golden rule of saving: Before paying bills or splurging, set aside a portion of your income for savings. Treat it as your most important bill—investing in your future self is priceless.

Take Advantage of Bank Technology: Banks are tech hubs that can boost your saving habit. Use apps to track spending, set up automatic transfers to your savings account on payday, and get alerts for your financial goals.

Pay Bills on Time and Pay More Than the Minimum: Avoid late fees and interest charges by staying on top of your bills and paying more than the minimum. This reduces debt faster and frees up money for savings.

Determine Needs Versus Wants: Differentiate between needs (rent, food, utilities) and wants (latest smartphone, designer jacket). Before spending, ask yourself which category your purchase falls into.

Shop Around: There's always a deal to be found, whether it's for insurance, groceries, or clothes. Use comparison websites, coupon apps, and negotiate to save money.

Consider Investments: Look into investment options like stocks, bonds, or mutual funds to grow your money over time. Consult a financial advisor for personalized advice.

Consult Your Local Bank: Schedule a chat with a financial advisor at your local bank to discuss savings accounts, certificates of deposit, or retirement accounts like IRAs.

Make It a Group Effort: Team up with friends or family members who also want to save. Challenge each other, share tips, and celebrate milestones together.

Reward Yourself: Set aside a "fun fund" for treats when you hit saving milestones. These rewards make the journey enjoyable and sustainable.

Reflect and Adjust: Regularly review your saving habits. Adjust your strategies as needed to meet your goals. Stay flexible and willing to tweak your approach as life changes.

Automating your savings

Automating your savings is like putting your financial growth on autopilot. It's a simple yet powerful strategy that ensures you're consistently contributing to your savings goals without having to lift a finger each time. Here's why making your savings automatic is a game-changer and how to do it.

Benefits of Automating Your Savings

Consistency: The biggest advantage of automating your savings is the consistency it brings. By setting up automatic transfers, you're ensuring that a specific amount of money is saved regularly, without fail. This consistency is key to building your savings over time.

Simplicity: Once you set it up, you don't have to think about it again. There's no need to remember to transfer money or make deposits; it's all done for you. This simplicity removes barriers to saving, making it easier to stick to your goals.

Prioritization: By automating your savings, you prioritize your future needs over immediate wants. It's a commitment to your financial health, ensuring that saving isn't an afterthought but a foundational aspect of your budget.

Compounding Benefits: The sooner you start saving, the more you benefit from compound interest. Automating your savings helps you start earlier and take full advantage of compounding, significantly increasing your savings over time.

Reduces Temptation: When money is automatically moved to savings, it's out of sight, out of mind. This reduces the temptation to spend on non-essential items, making it easier to stick to your financial plan.

Strategies for Automating Your Savings

Direct Deposit Allocations: Many employers allow you to split your paycheck between different accounts. Allocate a portion of your paycheck to go directly into your savings account.

Scheduled Bank Transfers: Set up a recurring transfer from your checking to your savings account. Schedule it right after payday to ensure you save before you spend.

Use Apps and Tools: There are numerous apps and tools designed to automate savings. Some round up your purchases to the nearest dollar and save the difference, while others analyze your spending habits to save small amounts that won't be missed.

Automate Increases: As your income grows, automatically increase the amount you're saving. Many banks and apps allow you to schedule incremental increases to your savings contributions.
By automating your savings, you're not just planning for the future—you're actively building it. It's a hassle-free way to ensure you're always moving closer to your financial goals, one automated step at a time.

Ways to automate your savings

Automating your savings doesn't just streamline your financial routine—it fortifies your future wealth with minimal effort. Here are some foolproof ways to ensure your piggy bank isn't just getting fed but feasting:

Direct Deposit Magic: Use your paycheck's direct deposit feature to automatically divert a portion of your earnings straight into your savings account. It's like playing financial hide-and-seek with your future self, where the prize is a growing savings account.

The Round-Up Rodeo: Embrace apps that round up your transactions to the nearest dollar, funneling those digital pennies into your savings. It's the modern-day equivalent of saving loose change in a jar, except it's all digital, and you won't accidentally spend it on a vending machine snack.

Scheduled Bank Transfers: Set a calendar reminder for a monthly savings party where a portion of your checking account dances its way into your savings account. The best part? You only need to RSVP once, and the bank keeps the party going every month.

Incremental Increases: Commit to upping your savings game annually or whenever you get a raise. A small increase in what you save can lead to significant growth over time, proving that even the smallest steps can lead to a giant leap in your savings journey.

Bill Pay, But Make It Saving: Some bills are inevitable, but what if you treated your savings goal as a non-negotiable monthly bill? Set up an automatic transfer as if you're paying the most important creditor of all: your future self.

By automating your savings in these ways, you're not just planning for tomorrow; you're ensuring a wealthier, more secure future with every automated step.

Master Your Savings in 15 Minutes: A Quick-Start Guide
Savings don't have to be daunting or time-consuming. In fact, you can set the foundation for a robust savings plan in just 15 minutes with this straightforward strategy. Here's how:

Minute 1-3: Define Your Saving Goals

Minute 1: Jot down your immediate savings goals (think short-term: concert tickets, a new game, etc.).

Minute 2: Outline your medium-term goals (like saving for a car or college expenses).

Minute 3: Dream big and list your long-term goals (think retirement, owning a home).

Minute 4-6: Assess Your Current Financial State

Minute 4: Quickly review your current bank account balances.

Minute 5: Estimate your monthly income, including any allowances, job earnings, or gifts.

Minute 6: Tally up your monthly expenses, including what you spend on entertainment, food outside of family meals, and other personal purchases.

Minute 7-9: Calculate Your Monthly Saving Potential

Minute 7: Subtract your expenses from your income to find out how much you can save each month.

Minute 8: Decide on a realistic percentage of your income that you want to save, aiming for at least 20% if possible.

Minute 9: Adjust your saving percentage based on your goals and financial review.

Minute 10-12: Choose Your Saving Tools

Minute 10: Pick a primary savings account for your long-term goals.

Minute 11: Consider opening a separate account or piggy bank for shorter-term goals to avoid dipping into long-term savings.

Minute 12: Research apps or bank features that can help automate your savings, like round-up savings apps or automatic transfers.

Minute 13-15: Set It Into Motion

Minute 13: Set up automatic transfers from your checking to your savings account based on your calculated saving potential.

Minute 14: Download any apps or tools you've chosen to aid your savings plan.

Minute 15: Mark a monthly check-in on your calendar to review your savings progress and adjust your plan as needed.

Segue

As we wrap up our journey through the essential world of saving, let's take a moment to reflect on the key takeaways from this enlightening chapter. From understanding the pivotal difference between saving and investing to embracing the power of starting early, we've navigated through the reasons why stashing away those dollars isn't just about preparing for a rainy day—it's about securing a future filled with possibilities.

Our journey into Investing 101 begins here. Here, we'll unlock the mysteries of the stock market, demystify bonds, and explore alternative investments, equipping you with the knowledge to make your money work for you. Expect to dive deep into strategies that seasoned investors use to grow their wealth, understand risk, and ultimately, become masters of their financial destiny.

So, stay tuned, keep that curiosity sparked, and let's continue to build not just arks, but entire fleets capable of navigating the future's uncertain waters with confidence and savvy. The journey to financial mastery is just beginning, and the next chapter promises to be an exhilarating part of this voyage toward empowerment and independence.

CHAPTER 6:

CRAFTING A WISE SPENDING BLUEPRINT

"*Spending money to show people how much money you have is the fastest way to have less money.*" – MORGAN HOUSEL

That is a story that hits closer to home than most would like to admit, especially in a society that values instant gratification and where swiping a card feels less like spending and more like a magic trick. Enter Jamie—a college student whose financial reality was a jigsaw puzzle of impulsive buys, late-night snack runs, and a "treat yourself" mantra that treated her bank account more like a revolving door than a reservoir of hard-earned cash.

Jamie's journey from a spendthrift to a sage spender mirrors the pitfalls many young adults face. Initially, her spending was all fun and games, a way to fit in, to celebrate the little wins—a coffee here, a pair of shoes on sale (but not really needed) there. However, the charm of impromptu purchases wore thin as the consequences piled up: a mountain of debt, the constant stress of making ends meet, and the gut-wrenching realization that her financial habits were barricading her from her true goals and aspirations.

The turning point came one bleak evening amidst a sea of bills and a bank statement that read more like a cry for help. It was then that Jamie realized the cost of her spending habits wasn't just monetary—it was costing her peace of mind, academic focus, and, most importantly, her future. That night, armed with a newfound resolve and a pen, Jamie outlined her battle plan.

She started with the basics—tracking her spending to the last penny, distinguishing needs from whimsical wants, and setting a budget that felt more like a lifeline than a leash. She swapped impulsive shopping sprees with mindful investments in her future, learning to derive joy not from the price tags but from the value her purchases brought to her life. She embraced the art of delayed gratification, discovering that the sweetest rewards often come to those who wait, plan, and spend wisely.

Jamie's story is a testament to the transformative power of intentional spending. It's a reminder that every dollar spent is a choice—a choice between fleeting pleasure and lasting fulfillment. Her journey from financial chaos to clarity and control is not just inspiring; it's a blueprint for anyone ready to rewrite their financial narrative. Through wise spending, Jamie found not just financial stability but a sense of personal empowerment and freedom that no impulsive purchase could ever offer.

Spending Needs vs. Wants: The Essential Guide

At the heart of savvy spending lies the critical distinction between needs and wants. Needs are your non-negotiables: shelter, groceries, basic clothing, and transportation costs. They're the pillars of your daily living. Wants, on the other hand, are your desires: that latest smartphone, designer shoes, or a dinner at a fancy restaurant. These are nice to have but not essential for survival.

Practical Examples
Needs: Rent, utility bills, a basic phone plan, groceries.

Wants: Subscription services, high-end sneakers, and the newest tech gadgets.

Pro Tip: Before making a purchase, ask yourself, "Can I live without this?" If yes, it's likely a want. Prioritize your needs to keep your finances in check and think twice before indulging in your wants.

Teen Spending Habits Unveiled
A Peek into Teen Wallets
The spending patterns of American teens reveal a dynamic interplay between necessity and luxury. On average, a teen spends about $2,331 annually, showcasing their active participation in the consumer world.

Where Does the Money Go?
Clothing: Teens allocate a significant chunk (20%) of their expenses to fashion, highlighting the importance of style and trends in their lives.

Food: Coming in close, food accounts for 19% of their spending, indicating a preference for dining out or grabbing snacks on the go.

Weekly Budget Breakdown: Teens manage a weekly budget of $44.8, combining contributions from parents ($26.9) and earnings from part-time jobs ($17.9). This blend of sources underscores the evolving financial landscape teens navigate as they balance dependence and independence.

Things Teenagers Waste Money On

Let's face it—we've all been guilty of splurging on stuff that makes our wallets cry in despair. But hey, knowledge is power, and recognizing these pitfalls is the first step to turning your financial ship around. So, what are these notorious cash sinks?

Food: Ah, the siren call of fast food and a grande latte. Easy on the taste buds, heavy on the pocket. Remember, every dollar you spend on that extra cheese pizza could be a brick in the empire you're building.

Clothing: Fashion fades, style is eternal, and so is the dent in your wallet if you're not careful. Chasing trends is like running on a treadmill; you spend a lot but don't get far. Invest in quality, not quantity.

Video Games: Gamers, hear me out. That new release might seem like the Holy Grail, but ask yourself, is it really worth the gold? Balance is key. There's a treasure in moderation.

In-app Purchases: Those little buys can add up to a mountain of cash. Remember, free-to-play doesn't mean free-to-spend. Keep your virtual spending in check, and your real-world treasury will thank you.

Makeup and Other Hygiene Products: Looking good is good business, but there's a fine line between investing in yourself and pouring money down the drain. Be wise about your beauty and hygiene purchases. Less is more if you choose wisely.

Listen, it's not about living like a hermit and swearing off all worldly pleasures. It's about being smart and making choices that reflect not just your current wants but also your future needs. As Warren Buffet wisely quipped, "Do not save what is left after spending, but spend what is left after saving." That's the kind of mindset we're aiming for.

Crafting a wise spending blueprint isn't rocket science—it's about being mindful, disciplined, and always keeping an eye on the prize. Your future self will thank you, and trust me, you'll be laughing all the way to the bank. Remember, every dollar you don't waste today is a soldier in your army of wealth tomorrow. Let's make them count!

Bad Spending Habits - Why Do You Overspend?

Ever wonder why your wallet feels like a sieve? It's those sneaky bad spending habits quietly draining your financial tank. Overspending often stems from a mix of emotional triggers (hello, retail therapy!), social pressures (keeping up with the Joneses, anyone?), and a lack of financial literacy. It's like being on a boat with a leak—if you don't find it and fix it, you're going to sink. Understanding the "why" behind your splurge fests is the first step in patching up your financial leaks and setting sail toward a more secure future.

Bad Spending Habits to Quit Today

Living Beyond Your Means: This one's a classic tale of financial folly. Trying to live like a Kardashian on a Bart Simpson budget? That's a recipe for disaster. If your lifestyle requires you to stretch your finances thinner than a slice of deli cheese, it's time for a reality check.

Overlooking the Significance of Budgeting: Ignoring budgeting is like driving blindfolded; you don't know where you're going until you crash. A budget is not just a boring spreadsheet—it's your financial roadmap. Without it, you're wandering in the dark.

Overspending on Nonessentials: Those little indulgences—a fancy coffee here, a spontaneous online purchase there—add up quicker than likes on a viral video. It's not about cutting out all joy from your life but about finding a balance. Ask yourself, "Do I need this, or do I just want it?" More often than not, you'll find your answer.

Quitting these habits won't happen overnight, but awareness is the first step. By recognizing these patterns, you can start to make changes. Think of your budget as a diet for your wallet; it's about making healthier choices, not starving yourself. Small, consistent changes can lead to big results. So, start today, and remember, the best time to plant a tree was 20 years ago; the second best time is now.

The Sneaky Culprits Behind Your Spending Sprees: Let's unravel the mystery behind those pesky spending habits that keep your bank account on a perpetual roller coaster. Understanding the "why" can light the path to nipping those habits in the bud.

Underestimating Expenses: Ever started the month thinking you've got your finances under control, only to end up wondering where all your money vanished? That's the classic case of underestimating expenses. It's the small leaks that sink the ship, from those "invisible" subscription fees to the daily gourmet coffees. Getting real with every penny that leaves your pocket can transform your financial landscape.

Peer Pressure and Social Media: In an era where lifestyle flaunting is just a scroll away, it's easy to fall into the trap of comparing your behind-the-scenes with everyone else's highlight reel. The fear of missing out (FOMO) can push you to spend on things you don't need to impress people you don't even like. Remember, social media is a curated display, not the full story.

Normalizing Debt: When swiping the credit card feels as routine as brushing your teeth, you've normalized debt. In a world where "buy now, pay later" is a common mantra, it's crucial to remember that debt is not a tool to inflate your lifestyle. It's a responsibility that can weigh you down if not managed wisely.

Emotional and Impulse Spending: Ever found yourself shopping online after a bad day? That's emotional spending. It's a temporary fix for emotional voids, leading to buyer's remorse. Recognizing this pattern is key to breaking the cycle. Before you click "buy," pause and ask, "Is this a need or a knee-jerk reaction?"

Discount Buying: Bargains can be a double-edged sword. It's easy to get swept away by the thrill of scoring a deal, buying things just because they're on sale, not because you need them. This "saving to spend" habit can ironically lead to more spending, cluttering your life with unnecessary possessions.

Peeling back the layers on these spending triggers reveals a common theme: mindfulness—or the lack thereof. By shining a light on these habits, you're already on the path to a healthier financial future.

Warning Bells: Signs You're on a Spending Spree

In the grand theater of life, your finances play a starring role. But when spending becomes the villain, it's time to sit up and take notice. Here are the flashing neon signs that your spending habits might be leading you down a slippery slope:

You Are Maxing Out Your Credit Cards: This is a glaring red flag. If your credit cards are always maxed out, it's like dancing on a financial tightrope without a safety net. Using credit cards isn't the issue; it's when they become a crutch for your spending that problems arise. It's like being in a boat that's taking on water—if you don't bail yourself out soon, you're going to sink.

You Are Making Impulse Purchases: Impulse buying is the financial equivalent of a sugar rush. It feels good in the moment but leaves you with a hangover of regret and a thinner wallet. If your purchases are more about instant gratification than actual need, it's a sign your spending habits need a health check.

Your Credit Score Decreased: A dropping credit score is like the silent alarm of your financial health. It's the universe's way of saying, "Hey, something's not right here." If your score is on a downward spiral, it's often due to high credit utilization or missed payments—both symptoms of spending issues.

You Don't Make Any Savings: The absence of savings is like trying to sail a ship without a compass; you might stay afloat, but you're not going anywhere. Saving is the cornerstone of financial stability. If you find it impossible to set aside even a small portion of your income, it's time to reassess your spending habits.

Recognizing these signs is the first step towards financial recovery. Just as a chain is only as strong as its weakest link, your financial security is only as robust as your spending habits. Addressing these issues head-on can transform your financial narrative from a cautionary tale to a success story. Remember, the goal isn't to stop spending but to start spending wisely.

Dodging the FOMO Spending Trap: Smart Strategies

In a world where the fear of missing out (FOMO) can lead to a drained bank account, it's crucial to arm yourself with strategies that help you dodge those peer pressure buys. Here's how you can stay financially fit while everyone else is splurging.

Limit Your Card Usage and Carry Cash: Switching to cash is like putting training wheels on your spending habits. It's harder to part with physical money than to swipe a card, making you think twice before making a purchase. This tangible connection to your spending can significantly reduce impulsive buys.

Suggest Free Alternatives: Who says fun has to drain your wallet? Next time the gang wants to splurge on an expensive outing, be the voice of reason and suggest a free or low-cost alternative. A picnic in the park, a home movie night, or exploring local free attractions can be just as enjoyable without the hefty price tag.

Lower Your Social Media Exposure: Social media is a highlight reel that can skew reality, making you feel left out and prompting unnecessary spending. Take a break or limit your scrolling time. Remember, comparison is the thief of joy—and often, the thief of financial peace.

Gratify Yourself Occasionally: It's not about a total spending freeze—it's about balance. Allow yourself occasional treats within reason. This way, you're not feeling deprived, which can often lead to binge spending later. Think of it as a diet; too strict, and you're bound to break it. Small, controlled indulgences can keep you on track without you feeling like you're missing out.

Halting the Habit: Strategies to Stop Impulse Buys Impulse buying is like a siren song for your wallet—enticing, mesmerizing, but potentially disastrous. Here are effective strategies to mute that call and steer your financial ship to safer waters:

Stick to a Shopping List: Before you venture into the treacherous waters of retail, arm yourself with a shopping list. This list is your anchor, keeping your spending focused on what you actually need rather than what momentarily catches your eye. Treating your shopping list as sacred can significantly reduce the temptation to stray into impulse purchase territory.

Reflect Before Purchasing: Implement a cooling-off period for purchases. If something catches your eye, give yourself 24 to 48 hours to think it over. This pause can drastically reduce the appeal of an impulse buy. Ask yourself, "Do I really need this, or is it just a fleeting desire?" This reflection can be a powerful antidote to impulsive spending.

Get to the Bottom of Your Impulse Spending Habit: Understanding the emotional or psychological triggers behind your impulse spending is crucial. Are you shopping out of boredom, stress, or to fill an emotional void? Recognizing these triggers can help you address the root cause and develop healthier coping mechanisms.

Create a Budget: A budget isn't just about tracking expenses—it's a tool for gaining financial freedom. Allocating specific amounts for different spending categories helps you prioritize your financial goals and limits the room for impulsive decisions. Seeing where your money is going can be a real eye-opener and a catalyst for change.

Create a Financial Goal: Having a clear financial goal gives your money a purpose beyond the immediate satisfaction of impulse buys. Whether it's saving for a vacation, building an emergency fund, or investing in your future, a tangible goal can motivate you to think twice before spending mindlessly.

Navigating the Digital Temptation: Tips to Curb Online Impulse Buys

In the digital age, where shopping is just a click away, resisting online impulse buys requires a mix of self-discipline and savvy strategies. Here's how to keep your online shopping habits in check and your finances on track.

Unsubscribe from Marketing Emails: Retailers are masters at tempting you with emails about sales and new arrivals. Take control by unsubscribing from these marketing lists. Out of sight, out of mind.

Install Ad Blockers: Ads are designed to lure you into buying things you didn't even know you wanted. Using ad blockers on your browser can minimize these temptations, keeping your online experience focused.

Set Up a Waiting Period
Implement a self-imposed rule: Wait at least 24 hours before making any online purchase. This cooling-off period helps differentiate between genuine needs and fleeting wants.

Use Website Blockers: If there are specific websites you can't resist, consider using website blockers during your vulnerable moments. These tools can prevent access to sites where you're likely to make impulse purchases.

Reflect on Past Purchases: Regularly review past impulse buys and the feelings associated with them. This reflection can highlight the emptiness of such purchases, reinforcing your resolve to stop.

Your Weekly Spending Log: Tracking Needs vs. Wants
Embark on a journey to financial clarity and responsibility by maintaining a weekly spending log. This simple yet effective tool will help you

distinguish between your needs and wants, providing insights into your spending habits and opportunities for improvement. Here's a blank template to get you started. Feel free to customize it to suit your lifestyle and financial goals.

Day of the Week	Date	Item Description	Category (Need/Want)	Amount ($)
Monday				
Tuesday				
Wednesday				
Thursday				
Friday				
Saturday				
Sunday				
Total			Needs:	
			Wants:	

Instructions:

- **Fill in the Date:** Start with the current week, ensuring you log each day's expenses.

- **Item Description:** Briefly describe what you spent money on.

- **Category:** Label each expense as a "Need" (essentials for living) or a "Want" (non-essentials).

- **Amount:** Note down how much you spent.

At the end of the week, tally up your total spending on Needs vs. Wants. This practice will illuminate where your money is going and encourage mindful spending. Remember, the goal isn't to judge yourself but to become more aware and intentional with your finances. Happy tracking!

Segue

As we wrap up this insightful journey through Chapter 6, "Crafting a Wise Spending Blueprint," let's take a moment to reflect on the key takeaways. We've navigated through the treacherous waters of spending pitfalls, from the allure of impulse buys to the societal pressures of FOMO spending.

Equipped with practical strategies and a newfound awareness, you're now poised to make intentional choices that align with your values, financial goals, and long-term aspirations.

Remember, mastering your spending habits isn't about deprivation—it's about empowerment. By understanding the significance of mindful spending and incorporating tools like weekly spending logs, you're setting the stage for a future where financial stability and peace of mind are your constant companions.

As we close this chapter, the curtain rises on an equally important aspect of your financial journey: "Building Your Savings Muscle." Expect to dive into the art of saving with purpose and precision. We'll explore how to transform your newfound spending wisdom into a robust savings strategy, turning today's disciplined choices into tomorrow's financial freedom.

Stay tuned for an enlightening expedition into the world of savings, where each dollar saved is a step closer to achieving your dreams. Let your curiosity lead the way as we continue to build a solid foundation for your financial future.

CHAPTER 7:

WEALTH BUILDING MADE EASIER

"*When you invest, you buy a day you don't have to work.*
—Duncan Williams

We're about to embark on a journey into the exhilarating investing world. This ain't your grandma's savings account; we're talking about making your money work so hard for you that it breaks a sweat. We're here to lift the veil on the mystique of the stock market, the allure of real estate, and the charm of bonds. By the end of this chapter, you'll be equipped with the know-how to navigate the investment landscape like a pro, making decisions that aren't just smart but downright genius. Let's turn those financial dreams into reality and get you on the fast track to a life where working is optional. Buckle up, it's going to be an epic ride!

Risk vs. Return

In the investing world, "risk vs. return" is the game's name. It's like the yin and yang of finance, where risk is the adrenaline-pumping roller coaster, and return is the sweet reward. Understanding this tradeoff is crucial because, let's face it, nobody wants to bet the farm on a whim.

The risk-return tradeoff tells us that the higher the potential return, the higher the risk. It's like choosing between a wild, unpredictable stallion and a steady, reliable workhorse. High-risk investments, like stocks, can gallop toward high returns, but they can also buck you off without warning. On the flip side, low-risk investments, like bonds or savings accounts, are more like a leisurely carriage ride—slower, but with fewer bumps along the way.

Why is this important? Because knowing your risk tolerance is like knowing your alcohol limit—it keeps you from waking up with a financial hangover. By understanding the risk-return tradeoff, you can craft an investment portfolio that suits your risk appetite, financial goals, and your dreams for the future.

It's about finding that sweet spot where you can sleep soundly at night while your investments quietly work their magic. So, let's dive in and master the art of balancing risk and return, turning you into a savvy investor who knows how to play the game and win.

Diversification: Spreading Your Financial Wings

Imagine you're at a buffet. You wouldn't pile your plate with just one dish, right? You'd sample a bit of everything to enjoy a balanced meal. That's diversification in a nutshell—it's about spreading your investments across different assets to create a balanced financial feast.

What's Diversification?

Diversification is the investment equivalent of not putting all your eggs in one basket. It's a strategy to reduce risk by investing in a variety of assets. This way, if one investment takes a nosedive, you've got others to cushion the fall. It's like having a safety net that catches you when one of your financial tightropes snaps.

Types of Diversification

Asset Class Diversification: This involves spreading your investments across different asset classes, such as stocks, bonds, and real estate. Each class reacts differently to market changes, so when one zigs, the other might zag.

Geographical Diversification: Why limit yourself to your own backyard? Investing in markets around the world can protect you from regional downturns and tap into global opportunities.

Sector Diversification: The market is a mosaic of technology, healthcare, and energy sectors. By investing in different sectors, you can shield yourself from the ups and downs of any single industry.

Reasons to Diversify Your Portfolio

Reduces Risk: Diversification is your financial shock absorber. It helps reduce the impact of a poor-performing investment on your overall portfolio.

Enhances Returns: By tapping into different investment opportunities, you increase your chances of hitting that sweet spot of higher returns.

Provides Stability: A well-diversified portfolio tends to be more stable, smoothing out the bumps in the market road.

Strategies to Diversify Your Portfolio
Start with a Solid Foundation: Begin with a mix of stocks, bonds, and cash that aligns with your risk tolerance and financial goals.

Branch Out: Explore different sectors, industries, and geographic regions to widen your investment horizon.

Keep an Eye on Balance: Regularly review and rebalance your portfolio to ensure it aligns with your diversification strategy.

Consider Mutual Funds and ETFs: These can offer instant diversification, as they hold a basket of different investments.

Diversification is your best bet for playing it smart in the grand casino of investing. It's about having a well-rounded portfolio that can weather the storms and sail smoothly toward your financial goals. So, spread your wings, diversify your investments, and watch your wealth grow harmoniously.

The Power of Compounding: Your Financial Growth Engine

Albert Einstein once called compound interest the "eighth wonder of the world," and for good reason. Compounding is the secret sauce that can turn a modest investment into a mountain of wealth over time. Let's dive into the magic of compounding and how you can harness its power to turbocharge your investments.

What's Compound Growth?: Compound growth is like a snowball rolling down a hill, gathering more snow and momentum. In the financial world, it means earning interest on your interest and the principal amount. It's not just growth—it's growth on growth.

How Compounding Works: Imagine you invest $1,000 at an annual interest rate of 5%. In the first year, you earn $50 in interest, totaling $1,050. In the second year, you earn interest on the new total of $1,050, resulting in $52.50 in interest and a new total of $1,102.50. This process continues, with the interest earning interest, leading to exponential growth.

Benefits of Compounding Over Time: The longer you let your investment compound, the more dramatic the growth. It's like planting and watching a seed grow into a mighty tree. The key is to start early and let time work magic, transforming small, regular investments into a substantial nest egg.

The Role of Time in Compounding: Time is the most crucial ingredient in the compounding recipe. The more time your money has to compound, the more significant the growth. Starting to invest early, even with smaller amounts, can lead to far greater wealth than starting later with larger sums.

Maximizing the Power of Compounding – Strategies

Start Early: The sooner you start investing, the more time your money has to compound.

Reinvest Your Earnings: Instead of pocketing your interest or dividends, reinvest them to supercharge your compounding engine.

Increase Your Contributions: Regularly increasing your investment amount can significantly boost your compounding potential.

Choose Investments with Higher Returns: While higher returns come with higher risks, carefully selected investments with higher potential returns can accelerate compounding.

Stay Invested: Resist the temptation to withdraw your money. The power of compounding shines brightest when you let your investment grow uninterrupted.

Overcoming Common Obstacles to Compounding

Impatience: Compounding takes time. Resist the urge for quick wins and focus on the long-term game.

Inconsistency: Regular contributions are key. Set up automatic transfers to ensure you consistently invest.

Fear of Risk: While being cautious is essential, being overly risk-averse can limit your returns. Find a balance that suits your risk tolerance.

Neglecting to Rebalance: As your investments grow, regularly rebalance your portfolio to ensure it aligns with your goals and risk tolerance.

Ignoring Fees: High fees can eat into your compounding gains. Look for low-cost investment options to maximize your returns.

The power of compounding is a force to be reckoned with in investing. By understanding how it works and implementing strategies to harness its potential, you can set yourself on a path to financial growth and prosperity.

What to Invest In: A Teen's Guide to Growing Wealth

Alright, young guns, let's dive into the investment buffet and see what's cooking. Each dish has its flavor, so let's break it down, giving you the lowdown on the good, the bad, and the potential for your greenbacks.

Funds (Mutual Funds & ETFs)

Bright Side: Diving into funds is like joining a rock band where each member brings a unique sound. Mutual funds and ETFs pool your money with other investors', managed by rockstar professionals aiming for the charts. They're a one-stop shop to diversify without playing every instrument yourself.

Stormy Side: Remember, even rockstars have off days. Fees can eat into your profits, and performance can vary. Not all funds are created equal, so tune your ear to find harmony in the chaos.

Savings Account
Bright Side: The classic hit of the financial world. A savings account is as steady as a drumbeat, offering a safe space for cash with some interest to sweeten the deal. Perfect for stashing your gig money with minimal fuss.

Stormy Side: Low interest rates might leave you stuck in the opening act forever. Inflation can outpace your earnings, slowly eroding the purchasing power of your savings.

Stocks
Bright Side: Stocks are the electric guitar of investing—high energy with potential for solos that bring the crowd to their feet. Investing in companies you believe in can lead to impressive gains and dividends.

Stormy Side: But, beware of feedback. Stocks can be volatile, with prices swinging wildly on market whims. It's a high-octane performance that's not for the faint of heart.

Custodial Account
Bright Side: For the underage virtuosos, a custodial account lets a guardian manage investments until you're ready to take the lead. It's a great way to learn the ropes and build wealth early.

Stormy Side: Once you're of age, the account is all yours, for better or worse. Ensure you're ready to solo, or your financial harmony could become a cacophony.

Plans (529 Plans for Education)

Bright Side: Think of 529 plans as your ticket to the main stage of education. These plans offer tax-advantaged savings for college, letting you amp up your education fund.

Stormy Side: They're a bit of a one-hit wonder, though. Use the funds for anything other than education, and you'll face taxes and penalties, cramping your style.

Roth IRA

Bright Side: The Roth IRA is like a royalty deal on your music. You pay taxes upfront, but your withdrawals in retirement are tax-free. It's a smooth track to financial freedom in your golden years.

Stormy Side: There's a cap on how much you can contribute each year, and high earners might hit a limit. It's a long play—withdraw early, and you could face penalties.

Bonds

Bright Side: Bonds are the ballads of the investing world—less dramatic but dependable. Lending money to governments or corporations can provide steady, if unspectacular, returns.

Stormy Side: The trade-off for stability is lower potential returns. Inflation can outpace bond earnings, turning your hit into a B-side.

Securities Account

Bright Side: A securities account gives you a backstage pass to the investment show, offering a platform to buy and sell stocks, bonds, and more. It's your toolkit for building an investment portfolio.

Stormy Side: With great power comes great responsibility. It's easy to get overwhelmed without a clear strategy or to make impulsive trades that don't align with your long-term goals.

Invest in Businesses

Bright Side: Whether through crowdfunding or starting your own, investing in businesses can be like headlining your show. The potential for growth and profits can be enormous.

Stormy Side: But remember, many bands break up before hitting it big. It's risky, with many variables out of your control. Ensure you're ready for the rollercoaster ride of entrepreneurship.

A smorgasbord of investment options, each with its flavor. Diversification is the key to a well-balanced portfolio—don't put all your eggs in one basket. Do your homework, start small, and keep learning. Investing is your oyster, so go ahead and crack it open!

Tips for Beginner Investors

Here are some tips to help you rock the stage as a beginner investor:

Educate Yourself: Knowledge is power; in the investment world, it's your backstage pass. Read books, follow financial blogs, and maybe even take a course or two. The more you know, the better your investment decisions will be.

Start Small, Dream Big: You don't need a platinum record to invest. Begin with small amounts and gradually increase as you get more comfortable. Remember, even the biggest bands started in small clubs.

Diversify Your Portfolio: Don't put all your eggs in one basket. Spread your investments across different assets to reduce risk. It's like having a setlist that appeals to all tastes.

Set Clear Goals: Are you saving for a world tour or a new guitar? Define your financial goals and invest accordingly. This will help you stay focused and make informed decisions.

Keep Emotions in Check: The market can be as volatile as a rockstar's mood. Don't let fear or greed drive your decisions. Stick to your strategy and stay cool under pressure.

Review Regularly: Like tuning your instrument, review your investments to ensure they align with your goals. Make adjustments as needed to keep your financial performance on track.

Don't Be Scammed: Avoiding Investment Frauds

The investment world can be a jungle, and predators are lurking. Here's how to avoid falling victim to investment fraud and scams:

Do Your Homework: Research any investment opportunity and the people behind it. If it sounds too good to be true, it probably is, like a free backstage pass.

Verify Credentials: Ensure that the financial advisor or firm you're dealing with is registered and licensed. It's like checking the credentials of a concert promoter.

Beware of High-Pressure Tactics: Scammers often use high-pressure tactics to rush you into making decisions. Take your time; don't let anyone push you into an investment.

Watch for Red Flags: Be wary of guaranteed returns, overly consistent performance, or complex strategies that are hard to understand. These are warning signs of a potential scam.

Keep Your Information Safe: Guard your personal and financial information like your prized guitar. Don't share it with anyone you don't trust.

By staying informed and vigilant, you can rock your investment journey while avoiding scams and fraud. Keep your eyes open, your mind sharp, and your investments secure.

Investment Mistakes to Avoid

Ah, the investment world—a place where fortunes are made and lost with the flick of a wrist. It's like a high-stakes poker game—you might bet the farm on a pair of twos if you're not careful. Here are some common investment mistakes you'll want to dodge faster than a bad record deal:

Chasing Hot Tips: Listening to the latest "hot tip" from your buddy or a random internet guru is like taking guitar lessons from a tone-deaf koala. Do your research and trust your due diligence over hearsay.

Ignoring Fees: Those little fees can nibble away at your returns like a backstage buffet. Pay attention to the costs associated with your investments, because every penny counts in the long run.

Letting Emotions Rule: Investing based on emotions is like trying to play a guitar solo with your feet—it's a bad idea. Stay calm, stick to your strategy, and don't let market ups and downs throw you off your game.

Forgetting to Diversify: Putting all your money in one investment is like betting your entire career on a single song. Spread your bets across different assets to reduce risk and keep your financial portfolio in tune.

Neglecting to Review Your Portfolio: Your investments need regular check-ups, like your guitar needs tuning. Review and adjust your portfolio periodically to align with your goals and risk tolerance.

Falling for Get-Rich-Quick Schemes: If an investment sounds too good to be true, it probably is. There's no shortcut to wealth, so be wary of schemes promising instant riches.

By steering clear of these common pitfalls, you'll be well on your way to mastering the art of investing.

Making the Investment Decision

It's time to get down to the nitty-gritty of making those investment decisions. It's like choosing the perfect setlist for your debut concert— you've got to pick the tunes that'll get the crowd roaring and keep them coming back for more.

Tune into Your Investment Ideas: Start by brainstorming a list of potential investments. Think of it as your financial playlist—what songs (investments) do you want to include? Consider stocks, bonds, real estate, or even starting your side hustle.

Hit the High Notes: Potential Returns. Now, let's talk potential returns, the headliners of your investment show. Research each investment idea to estimate how much money you might make. Remember, high returns often come with high risk, so don't get seduced by the promise of overnight success.

Face the Music: Assess the Difficulty. Not all investments are created equal. Some require more time, effort, or expertise than others. Assess the difficulty involved in each investment—is it a solo acoustic performance or a full-blown orchestral piece?

The Encore: Compare and Contrast. With your potential returns and difficulties in mind, it's time for the encore. Compare your investment ideas side by side. Which ones strike the right chord with your financial goals and risk tolerance?

Take the Stage: Make Your Choice. After weighing your options, it's time to take the stage and make your investment decision. Choose investments that harmonize with your financial aspirations and align with your risk appetite.

Investing is a personal journey, and there's no one-size-fits-all approach. Like in music, what works for one person might not work for another. Trust your instincts, stay informed, and don't be afraid to experiment.

With the right investments, you'll be well on your way to headlining the financial success festival. Let's rock this!

Segue

As we wrap up this rollercoaster ride through Chapter 7, "Wealth Building Made Easier," let's take a moment to soak in the financial wisdom we've jammed with. We've strutted through the basics of investing, grooved with risk and return, and jived with diversification. We've even learned to avoid hitting a bum note with investment scams and mistakes.

Investing is like learning a new instrument—it takes practice, patience, and a bit of soul. It's not about overnight success but about laying down a track leading to long-term wealth. So, keep your eyes on the prize, your mind open, and your investments in tune with your goals.

Hold onto your hats because we're about to dive into the next chapter, "Mastering the Art of Saving." Think of it as the B-side to our investment album. We will explore the secrets of saving that will multiply your money like fans at a sold-out show. We'll cover everything from emergency funds to saving for your dreams. So, stay tuned, stay excited, and let's keep building that financial empire, one smart move at a time. Let the savings begin!

CHAPTER 8:

NAVIGATING DEBT AND CREDIT SCORES

"*Remember this: debt is a form of bondage. It is a financial termite.*" – JOSEPH P. WIRTHLIN

Meet Juan, a college student juggling the high-wire act of academia and finances. With a backpack full of dreams and pockets weighed down by college loans and burgeoning credit card balances, Juan's journey is a tale of financial highs and lows. The thrill of independence quickly turned into a stress-filled saga, as each swipe of the card and each semester's tuition bill cast a longer shadow over Juan's future.

The turning point came when Juan realized that the shackles of debt weren't just a financial burden but a barrier to academic success and personal well-being. It was time to break free. Armed with determination and a newfound understanding of debt management, Juan embarked on a mission to consolidate debts and craft a strategic repayment plan.

The journey wasn't easy. It required discipline, sacrifices, and a steadfast commitment to responsible credit practices. But as the debts dwindled, so did the stress. Financial health gradually improved, and with it, the freedom to focus on academic pursuits and future aspirations.

The story of Juan is a beacon of hope, a testament to the power of smart debt management. It's a reminder that while debt can be a daunting foe, with the right strategies and mindset, it's a battle that can be won.

Shocking Statistics About Young Adults and Debts

The numbers are staggering—young adults are sinking in a sea of debt. From student loans to credit card bills, the financial burden is heavy, with many feeling like they're drowning with no lifeline in sight. Here are some eye-opening statistics:

Student Loan Debt: As of 2021, over 44 million Americans are saddled with student loan debt, totaling a staggering $1.7 trillion. The average student loan borrower graduates with around $30,000 in debt, a hefty price tag for education.

Credit Card Debt: A 2020 survey revealed that nearly 52% of millennials (ages 24-39) are bogged down by credit card debt, with many citing daily expenses and emergencies as the primary culprits.

Auto Loans: The average auto loan debt for millennials stands at approximately $18,200, as the allure of shiny, new vehicles often overshadows the financial burden they impose.

Living Paycheck to Paycheck: A 2019 report showed that a whopping 70% of millennials are living paycheck to paycheck, struggling to make ends meet, let alone save or invest.

These numbers paint a grim picture, but here's the silver lining: this chapter is your financial lifeboat. It's packed with strategies, tips, and wisdom to help you break free from the debt trap and steer your financial ship toward calmer waters.

You're not doomed to be a statistic; you're destined to be a success story. With the right knowledge and tools, you can turn the tide on debt and chart a course toward financial stability and freedom. So, let's roll up our sleeves and get to work. Your future self will thank you!

Bad vs. Good Debt – What's the Difference?

In the financial world, not all debt is created equal. There's the kind that drags you down like an anchor, and then there's the kind that can be a sail, propelling you forward. Let's break it down:

Bad Debt: This is the villain in your financial story. It's debt that doesn't contribute to your wealth or future income. Think high-interest credit card debt for that impulse shopping spree or a loan for a fancy car that depreciates faster than a rock star's fame. Bad debt is like a hole in your pocket—it keeps draining your resources without giving anything back.

Good Debt: Here's the hero. Good debt is an investment that can grow in value or generate long-term income. It's the student loan that leads to a higher-paying job, the mortgage for a home that appreciates over time, or the business loan that helps you launch or expand a profitable venture. Good debt is like a seed—with the right care, it can grow into a financial tree.

Borrowing – The Brighter and Darker Side

The Brighter Side: Borrowing can be a powerful tool when used wisely. It can help you seize opportunities, invest in your future, and achieve your financial goals. Loans can make education, homeownership, and entrepreneurship accessible, laying the foundation for a brighter financial future.

The Darker Side: However, borrowing has its pitfalls. Too much debt can lead to financial strain, stress, and even bankruptcy. High interest rates and fees can turn a manageable loan into a financial nightmare. It's essential to borrow within your means and have a solid repayment plan.

Debt is a double-edged sword. The key is to wield it wisely, using it to create opportunities and build wealth, rather than letting it control you. Be a financial ninja—strategic, mindful, and always on guard against the dangers of excessive borrowing.

Alternatives to Student Loans: Charting a Debt-Free Path to Education

Scholarships: These are the golden tickets of college funding. Scholarships are awarded based on various criteria, including academic achievement, athletic prowess, artistic talent, or community involvement. The best part? They don't need to be repaid. Start your treasure hunt early, and apply for as many as you can.

Grants: Similar to scholarships, grants are essentially free money for college. They're often need-based, so your financial situation could qualify you for this gift that keeps on giving. Check out federal grants like the Pell Grant, state grants, and those offered by your prospective college.

Work-Study: Get a job on or near campus that not only puts cash in your pocket but also complements your studies. The Federal Work-Study program provides part-time jobs for undergraduate and graduate students with financial need, allowing you to earn money to help pay for education expenses.

Stipends: Some academic programs or internships offer stipends, which are fixed sums of money paid periodically for services or to defray expenses. While not as common as other options, they're worth looking into, especially for graduate or doctoral students.

Tuition Reimbursement: If you're already in the workforce, your employer might offer tuition reimbursement as a part of your benefits package. This means they'll pay for all or part of your tuition fees, provided you meet certain criteria, such as maintaining a specific grade point average or staying with the company for a certain period after graduation.

Tuition Waivers: Some colleges offer tuition waivers to students who meet specific criteria, such as being a resident of the state, a veteran, or a student pursuing a field with high demand. While it might not cover all your expenses, it can significantly reduce your tuition bill.

Other Ways to Reduce Higher Education Costs

Community College: Starting at a community college and then transferring to a four-year university can save you a bundle on tuition.

Online Courses: With the rise of online education, you can take advantage of lower-cost courses or even free ones offered by reputable institutions.

Living Off-Campus: Sometimes, living off-campus can be cheaper than on-campus housing. Just make sure to factor in transportation and other living expenses.

Accelerated Programs: Some colleges offer accelerated programs that allow you to complete your degree in a shorter time, saving you money on tuition and other fees.

"Contact Us for Support"
Navigating the maze of college funding can be overwhelming, but you don't have to do it alone. Reach out to your school's financial aid office, talk to your guidance counselor, or connect with organizations dedicated to helping students find alternative funding options. Remember, investing in your education is investing in your future, and there are ways to do it without the burden of student loans. Keep exploring, stay informed, and take control of your financial destiny!

Credit Card Best Practices: Navigating the Plastic Jungle

Credit cards can be a double-edged sword—wield them wisely, and they're a tool for convenience and rewards; misuse them, and you're in a financial quagmire. Here's how to stay on the right side of the credit card game:

Read Your Card Agreement and Know Your Terms: Before you start swiping, get cozy with your credit card agreement. Understand the interest rates, grace periods, and any perks or penalties. Knowledge is power, and in this case, it's also money.

Be Aware of Any Fees You May Be Charged: Credit cards can come with a variety of fees—annual fees, late payment fees, foreign transaction fees, and more. Be aware of these potential charges and how to avoid them. Nobody likes nasty surprises on their bill.

Make Payments on Time: This one's a no-brainer but worth emphasizing. Late payments can lead to fees, higher interest rates, and a dent in your credit score. Set reminders or automate payments to ensure you're always on time.

Pay More Than the Minimum: Paying just the minimum keeps you in debt longer and racks up interest charges. Aim to pay off your balance in full each month, or at least chip away at it with more than the minimum payment.

Stay Below Your Credit Limit: Maxing out your credit card is a red flag for lenders and can hurt your credit score. A good rule of thumb is to keep your credit utilization—the amount you owe compared to your credit limit—below 30%.

Check Your Monthly Statements Carefully for Accuracy: Keep an eye on your statements for any errors or unauthorized charges. The sooner you catch and report these, the easier they are to resolve.

Report a Lost or Stolen Card Immediately: If your card goes missing, time is of the essence. Report it to your credit card issuer ASAP to prevent fraudulent charges and get a replacement card.

Credit Scores 101: Mastering the Numbers Game

In the financial symphony of life, your credit score is the lead violinist. It sets the tone for your financial credibility and dictates the rhythm of your borrowing journey. Let's dive into the world of credit scores, understand their composition, and learn how to conduct this vital aspect of your financial orchestra.

What's the Credit Score?

Picture this: Your credit score is like your financial GPA, a three-digit number that grades your creditworthiness. It's the magic number lenders use to decide whether to roll out the red carpet or show you the door. Ranging from 300 to 850, a higher score sings of reliability, while a lower score… well, let's just say it's a bit off-key.

This score is a snapshot of your credit report, which is a detailed record of your credit history. It includes your borrowing history, your punctuality in payments, the mix of credit you've used, and how much of your credit limit you're tapping into. In short, it's the sheet music that tells lenders how well you've been playing the financial tune.

Why Should You Improve Your Credit Score?

Elevating your credit score is like tuning your instrument before a big concert. A higher score can unlock lower interest rates, and better loan terms. And, it can even influence your insurance premiums and rental opportunities. It's the key to a smoother financial melody, reducing the cacophony of high interest rates and lending rejections.

Improving your score is not just about today—it's about setting the stage for your future financial endeavors. Whether you're eyeing a new car, or a home, or just want the peace of mind with financial flexibility, a symphonic credit score is your backstage pass.

How to Calculate Yours

Here's the twist: You don't calculate your credit score—the credit bureaus do. But you can conduct the factors that influence it. These maestros of credit, like Equifax, Experian, and TransUnion, use algorithms to translate your credit report into your score.

While the exact formula is as closely guarded as a celebrity's backstage, we know the main components:

Payment History (35%): Are you hitting the right notes by paying on time?

Amounts Owed (30%): How much of your credit are you using? Keeping this low is key.

Length of Credit History (15%): How long have you been playing in the financial orchestra?

Credit Mix (10%): A variety of credit types (credit cards, loans) can add depth to your score.

New Credit (10%): Opening new accounts can be a sharp note if done too frequently.

By understanding these factors and how they interplay, you can fine-tune your financial behaviors to hit the high notes and watch your credit score soar to symphonic heights.

Factors Affecting Your Credit Score

Payment History (35%): This is the heavyweight champion of your credit score. Late payments, bankruptcies, and defaults are the villains here. They can knock your score down faster than a house of cards in a hurricane.

Amounts Owed (30%): This is all about your credit utilization ratio. It's the percentage of your available credit that you're using. Keep it under 30% to show lenders you're not maxing out your cards like a shopaholic on Black Friday.

Length of Credit History (15%): This is the seasoned veteran of your credit score. A longer credit history provides a clearer picture of your financial habits, so don't close old accounts unless absolutely necessary.

Credit Mix (10%): Diversity is key here. A mix of credit cards, retail accounts, installment loans, and mortgages shows you can handle different types of credit like a financial maestro.

New Credit (10%): Opening several new credit accounts in a short period can raise red flags. It might look like you're desperate for credit, which is as appealing to lenders as a skunk at a garden party.

How to Build and Maintain a Stellar Score

Pay On Time, Every Time: Set up reminders or auto-payments to ensure you never miss a due date. A perfect payment history is like gold in the world of credit scores.

Keep Balances Low: Aim to use less than 30% of your available credit. It shows lenders you're not living on the edge of your credit limit.

Hold Onto Old Accounts: Older accounts add depth to your credit history. Think of them like fine wine—they get better with age.

Be Selective About New Credit: Don't apply for every credit card under the sun. Too many hard inquiries in a short period can ding your score.

Monitor Your Credit: Keep an eye on your credit report for errors or fraudulent activity. You can get a free report from each of the three major credit bureaus once a year at AnnualCreditReport.com.

Debt Reduction Worksheet: Your Roadmap to Financial Freedom

Get ready to tackle your debts head-on with this handy debt reduction worksheet. It's like a GPS for your finances, guiding you out of the red and into the black. Follow these steps, and you'll be waving goodbye to debt in no time!

Step 1: List Your Debts

Start by listing all your debts, including credit cards, loans, and any other amounts you owe. For each debt, note the following:
- Creditor Name
- Total Amount Owed
- Minimum Monthly Payment
- Interest Rate

Step 2: Rank Your Debts

Decide on a strategy for tackling your debts. You can go for the "Debt Snowball" method (paying off the smallest debts first for quick wins) or the "Debt Avalanche" method (targeting the debts with the highest interest rates first). Rank your debts in the order you plan to pay them off.

Step 3: Determine Your Monthly Payment
Figure out how much you can realistically pay toward your debts each month. This should be more than your minimum payments to make real progress.

Step 4: Allocate Payments
Start with the minimum payments for all debts. Then, allocate any extra funds to the debt at the top of your list (per your chosen strategy). Continue this monthly process, rolling over payments as you eliminate each debt.

Step 5: Monitor and Adjust
Keep track of your progress and update your worksheet regularly. As you pay off each debt, celebrate your success and then focus on the next one on your list.

Step 6: Stay Motivated
Keep your eye on the prize—a debt-free life! Visualize your goals, and remind yourself why you're working hard to reduce your debts.

By using this debt reduction worksheet as your financial compass, you'll navigate through the stormy seas of debt and sail into the calm waters of financial stability. Stay the course, and you'll reach your destination!

Creating a debt reduction worksheet is a great way to get organized and start tackling your debts. Here's a simple template you can use:

Debt Reduction Worksheet

Creditor Name	Total Amount Owed	Interest Rate	Minimum Monthly Payment	Extra Payment	New Payment	Remaining Balance
Example: Visa	$5,000	15%	$150	$50	$200	$4,800
Totals:						

Instructions

List all your debts: Fill in the creditor name, total amount owed, interest rate, and minimum monthly payment for each debt.

Decide on your extra payment: Determine how much extra you can pay toward your debts each month. This amount will be added to the minimum payment of the debt you're focusing on first.

Calculate your new payment: For the debt you're targeting first, add the extra payment to the minimum payment to get your new payment. For the other debts, the new payment is the same as the minimum payment.

Update your remaining balance: After making your payments, subtract the amount paid (minus interest) from the total amount owed to get your new remaining balance. Update this each month as you make payments.

Repeat the process: Once you've paid off one debt, move on to the next one on your list. Add the new payment from the paid-off debt to the minimum payment of the next debt, and continue the process until all debts are paid off.

This worksheet is a starting point. Feel free to customize it to fit your needs and financial situation. The key is to stay consistent with your payments and update the worksheet regularly to track your progress.

Segue

As we wrap up this journey through Chapter 8, "Navigating Debt and Credit Scores," let's take a moment to reflect on the financial wisdom we've unearthed. We've navigated the treacherous waters of debt, learning that it's not just about avoiding it like the plague but managing it like a pro. We've discovered that not all debt is a villain in disguise; some of it, when used wisely, can be a stepping stone to financial growth and prosperity.

We've also demystified the enigma that is the credit score, understanding that it's more than just a number—it's a reflection of our financial habits and discipline. We've armed ourselves with strategies to build and maintain stellar credit scores, ensuring that we remain attractive to lenders and unlock the doors to better financial opportunities.

But the journey doesn't end here, oh no. As we bid adieu to the world of debts and scores, we're about to dive headfirst into the next chapter: "Investing for the Future." It's time to shift gears from defense to offense, from saving ourselves from financial pitfalls to proactively building our wealth.

In the upcoming chapter, we'll explore the exciting realm of investments, from stocks and bonds to real estate and beyond. We'll learn how to make our money work for us, creating streams of passive income that flow into our financial reservoirs. We'll demystify the jargon, break down the barriers, and unveil the secrets to successful investing.

So, keep your financial compass handy and your curiosity ignited. The next chapter promises to be an exhilarating ride through the landscape of investments, where the potential for growth knows no bounds. Stay tuned, stay engaged, and let's continue to build a future that's not just financially secure, but downright prosperous. Onward to financial freedom!

CHAPTER 9:

RETIRE RICH, RETIRE HAPPY

"*In investing or retirement planning, TIME is your greatest asset.*" — FPS Insurance

Welcome to the grand finale of your financial symphony, Chapter 9: Retire Rich, Retire Happy. Picture this: You're sipping a cool drink on a beach without a care. That's not just a dream—it's a future you can create with smart retirement planning. This chapter isn't just about stashing away cash; it's about crafting a master plan that lets you live your golden years in style.

Retirement planning is like planting a tree. The best time to start was yesterday; the next best time is now. We're not just talking about saving money—we're talking about investing it wisely, creating multiple income streams, and ensuring you can live it up when you're older without worrying about every penny.

So, buckle up and get ready to dive into the nitty-gritty of retirement planning. We'll explore how to calculate how much you need, where to put your money, and how to make sure it lasts as long as you do. Let's make the dream of a happy, wealthy retirement a reality!

The Early Bird Catches the Worm: The Perks of Early Retirement Planning

To Enjoy the Benefits of Compound Interest: Compound interest is the magic ingredient in the recipe for a wealthy retirement. It's like a snowball rolling down a hill, gathering more snow and momentum as it goes. The earlier you start saving and investing, the larger your snowball grows, thanks to the power of compound interest. It's not just about what you save but how long your money has to grow. Starting early gives your investments more time to compound, turning small contributions into a substantial nest egg.

For a More Relaxed Transition into Retirement: Retirement should be a time of relaxation, not financial stress. By starting your planning early, you're paving the way for a smoother transition from the working world to retirement bliss. You'll have more time to fine-tune your investment strategies, adjust your savings goals, and ensure your retirement funds are on track. Think of it as a long, leisurely stroll to your retirement destination rather than a last-minute sprint.

Realize Your Dream of Early Retirement: Who says you have to wait until your 60s or 70s to retire? If you start planning and saving early, you might just be able to hang up your work boots sooner than you think. Early retirement is a dream for many, and it's achievable with disciplined savings, smart investing, and a clear vision of your retirement goals. The earlier you start, the more time you have to grow your wealth and make that dream a reality.

Saving Is Easier When You Have Sufficient Funds: Let's face it: Life can be unpredictable. By starting your retirement savings early, you're giving yourself a financial cushion for whatever comes your way. Whether it's an unexpected medical expense, a job loss, or a family emergency, having a solid retirement fund in place can provide peace of mind and financial security. Plus, the earlier you start, the less you have to save each month to reach your goals, making it easier on your budget.

The early bird doesn't just catch the worm—it catches financial freedom, peace of mind, and the freedom to retire on its own terms. So, don't wait for "someday" to start planning for your retirement. The time to start is now, and the rewards are well worth the effort. Let's get started on the path to a rich and happy retirement!

Risks of Not Planning for Retirement: Navigating the Perilous Path

Imagine sailing into the sunset of your life without a map or compass. That's what stepping into retirement without a plan can feel like. It's a journey fraught with uncertainty, and the stakes are high. Let's shed some light on the potential risks of not having a retirement plan:

Financial Insecurity: Without a retirement plan, you leave your financial future to chance. You might struggle to make ends meet, relying solely on Social Security or other limited income sources. The golden years you envisioned could turn into a period of financial strain, with limited options to improve your situation.

Reduced Quality of Life: Retirement should be a time to enjoy the fruits of your labor, not a time to pinch pennies. Without adequate savings, you might have to forego travel, hobbies, and other activities that bring joy and fulfillment. The lack of financial freedom can lead to a retirement more about survival than enjoyment.

Dependency on Others: Without a solid retirement plan, you might become financially dependent on family or friends. This can strain relationships and erode your sense of independence. It's a situation that many would prefer to avoid, yet it's a real risk for those who don't plan.

Limited Healthcare Options: Healthcare costs can skyrocket in retirement, especially as you age. Without sufficient savings, you might have to settle for lower-quality healthcare or forego necessary treatments. This can have a direct impact on your quality of life and longevity.

Forced to Work Longer: If you have yet to save enough for retirement, you might work well into your golden years, not by choice but by necessity. This can be physically and mentally taxing, especially if you're in a demanding job or facing health challenges.

Increased Stress and Anxiety: The uncertainty of an unplanned retirement can take a toll on your mental health. Worrying about finances can lead to stress, anxiety, and even depression, overshadowing what should be a peaceful and rewarding phase of life.

The risks of not planning for retirement are too significant to ignore. It's a journey that requires careful navigation, and the best time to start charting your course is now. By taking control of your retirement planning, you can avoid these risks and sail towards a secure and fulfilling future.

401(k) Tax Benefits: The Golden Egg of Retirement Savings

The world of 401(k) plans, where retirement savings isn't just smart but tax-savvy. This isn't just about stashing away cash for your golden years—it's about doing it in a way that makes Uncle Sam give you a thumbs up. Let's break down the tax benefits that make 401(k)s a retirement saver's best friend:

Pre-Tax Contributions: When you contribute to a traditional

401(k), that money comes out of your paycheck before taxes are applied. This means you're reducing your taxable income right off the bat. It's like getting a tax discount for doing something you should be doing anyway.

Tax-Deferred Growth: The money in your 401(k) doesn't just sit there—it grows over time through investments. The beauty of a 401(k) is that you don't pay taxes on that growth until you withdraw the money in retirement. It's like letting your money have a wild party without the taxman crashing it until much later.

Employer Match: Many employers offer a match on your 401(k) contributions, essentially free money. The best part? This match also enjoys the same tax-deferred status as your contributions. It's like getting a tax-free bonus just for saving for retirement.

Roth 401(k) Option: Some plans offer a Roth 401(k) option, where you contribute after-tax dollars, but your withdrawals in retirement are tax-free. This can be a great option if you expect to be in a higher tax bracket in retirement.

Loan and Hardship Withdrawals: While it's generally best to leave your 401(k) untouched until retirement, some plans allow for loans or hardship withdrawals in certain situations. While these can have tax implications, they can also provide a financial lifeline in emergencies.

A 401(k) is more than just a retirement savings plan; it's a tax-advantaged powerhouse that can help you maximize your savings and minimize your tax bill. By understanding and leveraging the tax benefits of a

401(k), you're not just planning for retirement but a richer, happier future. So, start contributing, and watch your retirement nest egg and tax savings grow!

Where to Build Your Egg Nest: Top Retirement Avenues for Teens

Roth IRA

Features: A Roth IRA is a retirement account where you contribute after-tax dollars and your withdrawals in retirement are tax-free.

Pros: Perfect for teens with part-time jobs, as it offers tax-free growth and withdrawals. Plus, you can withdraw your contributions (but not earnings) at any time without penalty.

Cons: There are contribution limits, and you can't deduct your contributions on your taxes.

Traditional IRA

Features: Contributions are often tax-deductible, and earnings grow tax-deferred until you withdraw them in retirement.

Pros: It can reduce your taxable income now, which is a bonus if you're in a higher tax bracket.

Cons: Withdrawals in retirement are taxed as regular income, and there are penalties for early withdrawals.

401(k) or 403(b) Plans
Features: Employer-sponsored retirement plans where contributions are made pre-tax, and earnings grow tax-deferred.

Pros: Many employers offer matching contributions, which is essentially free money for your retirement.

Cons: Limited investment options compared to IRAs, and early withdrawals come with penalties and taxes.

Health Savings Account (HSA)
Features: An account for individuals with high-deductible health plans, allowing for tax-free contributions, growth, and withdrawals for qualified medical expenses.

Pros: After age 65, you can use the funds for any purpose without penalty (though non-medical withdrawals are taxed).

Cons: You must have a high-deductible health plan to qualify, and there are contribution limits.

Brokerage Accounts

Features: Investment accounts that allow you to buy and sell a wide range of assets, from stocks to bonds to mutual funds.

Pros: No contribution limits and a wide range of investment options.

Cons: No tax advantages for retirement savings, and capital gains and dividends are taxed.

Real Estate

Features: Investing in property, either directly or through real estate investment trusts (REITs).

Pros: Potential for both rental income and property appreciation.

Cons: Requires significant capital, and there are risks associated with property management and market fluctuations.

Building your retirement nest egg as a teen is like planting a financial seed that can grow into a mighty oak. Each retirement avenue has unique features, pros, and cons, so choosing the one that aligns with your financial goals and circumstances is essential.

How Much Do You Need for Retirement? A Roadmap for Every Age

Retirement planning is like setting sail on a financial voyage. The amount you need to set aside depends on your desired destination, the length of your journey, and the lifestyle you want to maintain. Here's a breakdown of what you should consider at different stages of your life:

In Your 20s: The Foundation Years
Start Saving Early: Aim to save at least 10-15% of your income for retirement. The power of compound interest is your best friend at this stage.

Set Realistic Goals: Use retirement calculators to estimate how much you'll need based on your desired retirement age and lifestyle.

In Your 30s: Building Momentum
Increase Contributions: As your income grows, try to increase your retirement savings rate. Aim for 15-20% of your income.

Consider Lifestyle Factors: Think about your future lifestyle. Do you plan to travel? Downsize your home? These decisions will impact how much you need to save.

In Your 40s: Mid-Course Adjustments
Assess Your Progress: Check if you're on track to meet your retirement goals. If you're behind, consider increasing your savings rate or adjusting your investment strategy.

Factor in Health Care Costs: Health care can be a significant expense in retirement. Start factoring these costs into your savings goals.

In Your 50s: The Home Stretch

Maximize Contributions: Take advantage of catch-up contributions in your retirement accounts. The IRS allows individuals over 50 to contribute extra amounts to their 401(k) and IRA.

Fine-tune Your Strategy: Review your investment portfolio and ensure it aligns with your risk tolerance and retirement timeline.

In Your 60s: Preparing for Landing

Calculate Your Retirement Income: Estimate your income from Social Security, pensions, and retirement accounts. Ensure it aligns with your expected expenses.

Plan for Withdrawals: Develop a strategy for withdrawing from your retirement accounts to minimize taxes and ensure your savings last.

Factors to Consider

Life Expectancy: Plan for a long retirement. Many people live into their 90s, so ensure your savings can support you.

Inflation: Consider the impact of inflation on your purchasing power. Your retirement savings need to keep pace with rising costs.

Unexpected Expenses: Be prepared for unexpected costs like home repairs or medical expenses.

There's no one-size-fits-all answer to how much you need for retirement. It's a personalized journey that requires careful planning and regular adjustments. By starting early, saving consistently, and planning wisely, you can set the course for a retirement that's not just comfortable but truly enriching.

Planning for Retirement: Setting Your Sights on the Future

Retirement planning is like charting a course for a long-awaited voyage. It's about envisioning your destination and plotting the steps to get there. Let's break down how to set retirement goals and create a plan to guide you to a future of financial security and fulfillment.

What Are Retirement Goals?

Retirement goals are the financial objectives you aim to achieve by retirement. They are the backbone of your retirement plan, shaping your saving and investment strategies. These goals can range from maintaining your current lifestyle in retirement to fulfilling dreams like traveling the world or purchasing a vacation home.

How to Set Retirement Goals – Steps
Determining Your Sources of Income

Social Security: Estimate your Social Security benefits based on your work history and retirement age.

Pensions: If you're entitled to a pension, understand the terms and how much you can expect to receive.

Retirement Accounts: Calculate the potential value of your 401(k), IRA, or other retirement accounts by the time you retire.

Other Income: Consider other sources of income, such as rental properties, part-time work, or investments.

Creating a Retirement Savings Program

Start Early: The sooner you start saving, the more time your money has to grow.

Contribute Regularly: Set up automatic contributions to your retirement accounts to ensure consistent savings.

Maximize Contributions: Take advantage of contribution limits for retirement accounts, and make catch-up contributions if you're over 50.

Estimating Potential Retirement Expenses

Basic Living Expenses: Calculate your expected costs for housing, food, utilities, and transportation.

Healthcare Costs: Factor in the cost of healthcare, including Medicare premiums, out-of-pocket expenses, and long-term care.

Lifestyle Expenses: Consider the cost of hobbies, travel, and other activities you plan to enjoy in retirement.

Managing Risk

Investment Risk: Diversify your investments to manage risk and aim for a balanced portfolio that aligns with your risk tolerance.

Inflation Risk: Plan for inflation by investing in assets that have the potential to grow at a rate that outpaces inflation.

Longevity Risk: Ensure your retirement savings can support you for a potentially long retirement.

Managing Current and Future Assets

Review and Adjust: Regularly review your retirement plan and make adjustments based on changes in your life, the economy, or your goals.

Estate Planning: Consider how you want to manage and distribute your assets after you pass away. This may include creating a will, setting up trusts, or making other estate planning arrangements.

Setting retirement goals is crucial to securing a comfortable and fulfilling retirement. By carefully planning your income sources, savings strategy, and expenses, and managing risks and assets, you can create a roadmap leading to a financially secure and happy retirement.

15-Minute Retirement Planner

Step 1: Assess Your Current Financial Situation (3 minutes)

Net Worth: List your assets (savings, investments, property) and liabilities (debts, loans). Subtract liabilities from assets to get your net worth.

Income: Note down your current income sources and amounts.

Step 2: Define Your Retirement Goals (3 minutes)
Age of Retirement: Decide at what age you aim to retire.

Lifestyle: Envision the lifestyle you want in retirement (travel, hobbies, home).

Income Needs: Estimate your annual income to support your desired lifestyle.

Step 3: Estimate Your Retirement Income (3 minutes)
Social Security: Use the Social Security Administration's online calculator to estimate your benefits.

Pensions: If applicable, note down your expected pension income.

Retirement Accounts: Estimate the future value of your 401(k), IRA, or other retirement accounts based on current balances and contributions.

Step 4: Calculate Your Retirement Gap (2 minutes)
Subtract your estimated retirement income from your desired annual income to find your retirement gap. You'll need to cover this amount through additional savings or investments.

Step 5: Create a Savings and Investment Plan (2 minutes)
Savings Rate: Determine how much you need to save each month to close the retirement gap.

Investment Strategy: Decide on an investment strategy that aligns with your risk tolerance and time horizon.

Step 6: Review and Adjust (2 minutes)

Revisit Your Plan: Regularly review your retirement plan and adjust your savings rate or investment strategy as needed.

Stay Informed: Keep up to date with changes in retirement laws, investment options, and economic conditions that may impact your plan.

Bonus Tips

Maximize Retirement Account Contributions: Take advantage of tax-deferred or tax-free growth in retirement accounts like 401(k)s and IRAs.

Diversify Your Investments: Spread your investments across different asset classes to reduce risk.

Consider Professional Advice: A financial advisor can provide personalized guidance and help you navigate complex retirement planning decisions.

Following this 15-minute retirement planner can lay the groundwork for a solid retirement plan. Remember, the key to a successful retirement is starting early, being consistent with your savings, and regularly reviewing and adjusting your plan to stay on track.

CONCLUSION

Alright, rockstars of the financial world, we've reached the grand finale of our money-making, wealth-building, retirement-rocking journey. It's been a wild ride, but like all great gigs, it must come to an end. So, let's hit the high notes one last time and bring this show to a close.

The main message of this financial symphony is clear: Your money is a tool, a ticket to the life you've always dreamed of. It's not just about stacking cash—it's about creating a future that's rich in every sense of the word. We've explored the ins and outs of budgeting, saving, investing, and retirement planning. We've tackled debt, credit scores, and the power of compound interest. Each chapter was a chord in the melody that's leading you to financial freedom.

The golden nugget of wisdom we've been digging for is simple: Take control of your money before it takes control of you. It's about making your cash work for you, not the other way around. Whether it's through budgeting like a boss, investing like a pro, or planning for retirement like a visionary, the power to shape your financial future is in your hands.

Now, let's bring it home with the key takeaways that should be etched in your mind:

Budgeting is your foundation: Without it, you're building your financial house on sand.

Saving is your safety net: It's what keeps you from freefalling when life throws you a curveball.

Investing is your growth engine: It's how you turn your savings into a money-making machine.

Retirement planning is your ticket to a worry-free future: Start early, and you'll thank yourself later.

But hey, don't let the end of this book be the end of your journey. It's just the beginning, baby! Armed with the tools and insights from these pages, step out into the world with your financial confidence cranked up to eleven. Start making moves—budgeting, saving, investing, and spending wisely. Your financial destiny is yours to mold, like a potter with a lump of clay. Go out there and sculpt the future you've been dreaming of!

The key takeaway, the chorus that should be echoing in your mind, is this: Start today. Time is your most valuable asset, and the earlier you start managing your money wisely, the sooner you'll be living the life you've envisioned. Whether you're a fresh-faced newbie or a seasoned pro, there's always room to grow, learn, and improve your financial game.

Remember, wealth isn't just about having a fat bank account—it's about having the freedom to live on your terms. It's about waking up daily with a sense of abundance, knowing you're in control of your financial destiny. So, take the lessons from this book, apply them to your life, and watch your financial dreams become reality.

As you close this book and step back into the real world, carry with you the knowledge, the strategies, and the confidence you've gained. Keep pushing, keep growing, and never stop striving for that rich, happy

CONCLUSION

life you deserve. The stage is set, the lights are on, and it's your time to shine.

Don't forget, "It's not about the money; it's about your dreams." So go out there, chase those dreams, and make them a reality. Here's to your success, happiness, and unstoppable financial future. Rock on!

Picture this: A young entrepreneur named Alex, who once lived paycheck to paycheck, is drowning in debt. By applying the principles in this book, Alex turned the tide, paid off all debts, and started a thriving business. Today, Alex is financially stable and mentors others to achieve their financial dreams. That's the power of taking control of your finances!

Now, it's your turn. The journey doesn't end here—it begins. Armed with the tools and insights within these pages, step into the world with financial confidence. Start budgeting, saving, investing, and spending wisely. Your financial destiny is yours to shape. Go out there and build the future you deserve!

If this book has sparked a fire in you, if it's given you the tools to start your journey to financial freedom, I'd be honored if you left a review. Share your thoughts and successes, and let's inspire others to take control of their financial destinies. Together, we can build a world of financially savvy individuals, living life on their own terms. Here's to your success, and thank you for being a part of this journey!

ACKNOWLEDGMENTS

My deepest gratitude to my heavenly father
for the wisdom and guidance in my life.

Heartfelt thanks to my wife Priscila, my children
Micaiah, Jedidiah, and Anaiah, and all my
family for their unwavering support.

A special mention to Maria, Lisa, Emily, Rabia,
and the AIA community—your contributions have been invaluable in
bringing this book to life.
Thank you for your talent, dedication, and hard work.

ABOUT THE AUTHOR

Freddie Awuah-Gyasi is a compelling and insightful 38-year-old father of three, deeply committed to educating young minds in the realm of financial literacy. His journey through the intricate world of personal finance is grounded in both his robust academic background and his personal experiences with financial management as a family man.

With a Bachelor's in Physics and Computer Science from the University of Ghana and a Master's in Computer Science from Wake Forest University, NC, Freddie adeptly combines his technical expertise with practical financial know-how. This unique blend allows him to demystify complex financial concepts, making them accessible and engaging for teens and young adults.

Freddie's work in financial literacy is driven by his passion to empower the next generation with the knowledge and tools necessary for financial independence and success. His books on money management, budgeting, saving, and investing are not just informative but also resonate with real-life scenarios, making them invaluable resources for young readers.

Beyond his written work, Freddie is dedicated to the cause of financial education, often speaking and conducting workshops for young audiences. His approachable demeanor and ability to connect with his readers and listeners have made him a trusted voice in the field of youth financial education.

As a parent, Freddie understands the importance of instilling sound financial habits early on. His commitment to this cause is evident in his writing, which not only educates but also inspires young individuals to confidently navigate their financial futures. Freddie Awuah-Gyasi stands as a guiding figure, championing the empowerment of teens and young adults through financial literacy.

But divide your investments among many places, for you do not know what risks might lie ahead.
— *Ecclesiastes 11:2*

REFERENCES

1. The Total Money Makeover: A Proven Plan for Financial Fitness by Dave Ramsey

2. Rich Dad Poor Dad: What the Rich Teach Their Kids About Money That the Poor and Middle Class Do Not! by Robert T. Kiyosaki

3. The Millionaire Next Door: The Surprising Secrets of America's Wealthy by Thomas J. Stanley and William D. Danko

4. I Will Teach You to Be Rich by Ramit Sethi

5. Your Money or Your Life: 9 Steps to Transforming Your Relationship with Money and Achieving Financial Independence by Vicki Robin and Joe Dominguez

6. The Richest Man in Babylon by George S. Clason

7. The Index Card: Why Personal Finance Doesn't Have to Be Complicated by Helaine Olen and Harold Pollack

8. The Behavior Gap: Simple Ways to Stop Doing Dumb Things with Money by Carl Richards

9. The Automatic Millionaire: A Powerful One-Step Plan to Live and Finish Rich by David Bach

10. Broke Millennial: Stop Scraping By and Get Your Financial Life Together by Erin Lowry

11. Get a Financial Life: Personal Finance in Your Twenties and Thirties by Beth Kobliner

12. The Money Book for the Young, Fabulous & Broke by Suze Orman

13. Smart Money Smart Kids: Raising the Next Generation to Win with Money by Dave Ramsey and Rachel Cruze

14. Why Didn't They Teach Me This in School?: 99 Personal Money Management Principles to Live By by Cary Siegel

15. The Motley Fool Investment Guide for Teens: 8 Steps to Having More Money Than Your Parents Ever Dreamed Of by David and Tom Gardner

16. The Young Entrepreneur's Guide to Starting and Running a Business: Turn Your Ideas into Money! by Steve Mariotti

17. You Are a Badass at Making Money: Master the Mindset of Wealth by Jen Sincero

18. How to Turn $100 into $1,000,000: Earn! Save! Invest! by James McKenna and Jeannine Glista

19. The Teen Money Manual: A Guide to Cash, Credit, Spending, Saving, Work, Wealth, and More by Kara McGuire

20. The Opposite of Spoiled: Raising Kids Who Are Grounded, Generous, and Smart About Money by Ron Lieber

21. Make Your Kid a Money Genius (Even If You're Not): A Parents' Guide for Kids 3 to 23 by Beth Kobliner

22. How to Manage Your Money When You Don't Have Any by Erik Wecks

23. Clever Girl Finance: Ditch Debt, Save Money, and Build Real Wealth by Bola Sokunbi

24. The Art of Money: A Life-Changing Guide to Financial Happiness by Bari Tessler

25. Money Honey: A Simple 7-Step Guide for Getting Your Financial $hit Together by Rachel Richards

26. Financial Basics: A Money-Management Guide for Students by Susan Knox

27. The No-Spend Challenge Guide: How to Stop Spending Money Impulsively, Pay off Debt Fast, & Make Your Finances Fit Your Dreams by Jen Smith

28. Finance 101 for Kids: Money Lessons Children Cannot Afford to Miss by Walter Andal

29. The Financial Diet: A Total Beginner's Guide to Getting Good with Money by Chelsea Fagan and Lauren Ver Hage

30. Your Money Matters: 21 Tips for Achieving Financial Security in the 21st Century by Jonathan D. Pond

INDEX

SYMBOLS
15 minutes 10, 11, 102, 117
401(k) 171, 172, 173, 174, 177, 179, 181

A
achievement 23, 70, 154
Anxiety 171
aspirations 11, 81, 122, 134, 148, 152
ATM 73, 74, 75, 79, 80, 96, 97

B
bank 19, 22, 28, 31, 32, 34, 52, 59, 62, 67, 68, 72, 77, 78, 79, 80, 81, 82, 83, 84, 85, 86, 87, 93, 96, 97, 114, 116, 117, 118, 119, 121, 122, 125, 126, 129, 184
Bank 19, 47, 77, 78, 79, 85, 86, 90, 113, 114, 116, 117
bank account 10, 28, 59, 62, 85, 87, 118, 121, 126, 129, 184
banking 11, 67, 68, 71, 72, 73, 74, 75, 78, 81, 82, 83, 84, 85, 86, 87
Bills 21, 113
bonus 34, 172, 174
budget 11, 33, 36, 68, 89, 90, 91, 92, 93, 94, 95, 96, 97, 100, 103, 104, 112, 115, 122, 123, 125, 126, 131, 169
budget, 11, 92, 100
Budgeting 7, 29, 32, 33, 89, 90, 91, 92, 97, 98, 102, 126, 183

C
Central Banks 72
Checking Accounts 68, 73, 74
Coins 21
comfort 23
Community Banks 72
credit 11, 16, 19, 30, 33, 34, 36, 37, 68, 69, 78, 87, 88, 96, 101, 108, 127, 128, 151, 152, 153, 157, 158, 159, 160, 161, 162, 165, 183
Credit 7, 30, 34, 68, 88, 96, 128, 151, 152, 156, 157, 158, 159, 160, 161, 165
crossroads 10
cryptocurrencies 20
curveball 93, 184
cybersecurity 82

D
debit card 68, 70, 71, 74, 99
Debt 7, 16, 30, 33, 92, 108, 127, 151, 152, 153, 154, 162, 163, 164, 165
digital 11, 18, 19, 20, 22, 41, 42, 47, 49, 50, 51, 57, 62, 63, 64, 72, 75, 82, 85, 87, 98, 99, 117, 131
digital banking 11, 82
dough 19, 22, 38, 67, 97
dreams 9, 10, 18, 19, 23, 46, 55, 56, 57, 59, 73, 91, 92, 93, 98, 102, 109, 111, 134, 135, 136, 149, 151, 178, 184, 185

E
Empire 60
Empowerment 17, 32
Engage, Apply, and Master 11
entrepreneurship 43, 54, 66, 144, 154
exercises 11, 12

F

Fees 71, 74, 75, 79, 96, 141, 147, 157
financial 9, 10, 11, 12, 13, 14, 15, 16, 17, 19, 20, 21, 22, 25, 26, 27, 28, 29, 30, 31, 32, 33, 34, 35, 36, 37, 38, 39, 41, 42, 43, 45, 49, 50, 51, 53, 55, 59, 60, 61, 62, 64, 65, 66, 67, 68, 70, 71, 72, 73, 74, 75, 76, 78, 80, 81, 82, 83, 84, 85, 86, 87, 88, 89, 90, 91, 92, 93, 94, 95, 97, 98, 99, 100, 101, 102, 103, 104, 105, 106, 107, 108, 109, 112, 113, 114, 115, 116, 118, 120, 121, 122, 124, 125, 126, 127, 128, 129, 130, 131, 132, 133, 134, 135, 136, 137, 138, 139, 141, 142, 143, 144, 145, 146, 147, 148, 149, 151, 152, 153, 154, 155, 156, 157, 158, 159, 160, 161, 163, 165, 166, 167, 168, 169, 170, 172, 175, 176, 178, 182, 183, 184, 185
Financial Planning 30
Freddie Awuah-Gyasi 3, 4, 13, 17

G

game-changer 12, 38, 43, 81, 114
gift 34, 69, 94, 155
goal 9, 13, 43, 65, 94, 95, 101, 103, 106, 110, 117, 129, 131, 134
Golden Egg 171
Goldmine 42, 49

H

Healthcare 170, 179
high-interest 30, 33, 79, 110, 153

I

Income 42, 43, 51, 58, 59, 60, 61, 94, 103, 177, 178, 179, 180, 181
Investing 30, 33, 61, 105, 106, 119, 137, 142, 144, 147, 148, 149, 165, 175, 184
Investment Banks 72

M

making a living 25, 33
million 27, 152
Mindset 25, 26, 27, 28
Mo Money, Mo Problems 20
money 10, 11, 16, 18, 19, 20, 21, 22, 23, 24, 25, 26, 27, 28, 29, 30, 31, 32, 33, 34, 35, 36, 38, 39, 41, 42, 43, 44, 45, 46, 47, 49, 50, 51, 52, 53, 55, 59, 60, 61, 64, 65, 66, 67, 68, 69, 70, 71, 72, 73, 74, 75, 76, 77, 78, 80, 81, 82, 84, 85, 89, 90, 91, 92, 93, 94, 96, 97, 98, 99, 100, 101, 104, 105, 106, 107, 109, 110, 111, 112, 113, 114, 115, 120, 121, 125, 126, 129, 131, 133, 135, 139, 140, 141, 142, 143, 147, 148, 149, 155, 156, 157, 166, 167, 168, 172, 174, 179, 183, 184, 185
Money Management 55, 84
Money Skills 1, 3, 9, 29, 31, 32, 33
mortgage 30, 33, 154

O

Online Banking 75, 78, 81, 82, 86
Online Banks 72
online store 51, 60

P
password 83
piggy banks 20, 45
Plastic Money 21

Q
Quiz 34

R
Reputation 34, 78
Resilience 55

S
salary 34
Saving 7, 29, 32, 36, 54, 73, 105, 106, 107, 108, 109, 110, 111, 117, 118, 119, 128, 149, 169, 176, 184
Savings Accounts 70, 73, 76, 77
Scam 49
Skills 1, 3, 9, 13, 28, 29, 31, 32, 33, 44, 48
Skill Set 55
Spending 7, 16, 30, 94, 95, 103, 111, 112, 121, 122, 123, 125, 126, 127, 128, 129, 131, 132, 134
street cred 20
Stress 35, 59, 107, 171

T
Tax Benefits 171
teenagers 9
The Future is Yours 11
The Power of 15 Minutes 10
The Practical Toolkit 11
This Japanese proverb 15
TikTok 21, 47, 57, 78

U
United States 4, 9

W
wealth 25, 28, 32, 33, 39, 42, 60, 80, 98, 104, 106, 108, 116, 120, 125, 138, 139, 142, 147, 149, 153, 154, 166, 169, 183, 184

Y
Yin and Yang 73

YOUR REVIEW CAN LIGHT THE WAY!

Spark a Change with Your Words

"Every penny saved is a step towards your financial dreams. Sharing your journey can guide others to start their own." - Freddie Awuah-Gyasi

Did you know? Folks who share their wisdom not only enrich their own lives but also pave the way for others to flourish. And if we've got the chance to do just that together, you bet we're going to seize it!

Here's a thought I'd love for you to ponder...

Would you extend a helping hand to a stranger, even if no one ever found out it was you?

Imagine this person—they're probably a lot like you were at the beginning of your financial journey. Eager to learn, ready to make a change, but unsure of where to start.

Our mission is to make Money Skills for Teens and Young Adults a beacon for financial literacy for all. This mission serves as my motivation for every action I take. To truly make an impact, we need to reach... well, everyone.

And this is where you come in. It's no secret that people tend to judge a book by its cover (and what others say about it). So, on behalf of a future financial whiz you've yet to meet, I have a small request:

Could you share a review of this book?

It won't cost you a dime and will take less than a minute, but your review has the power to change another person's life profoundly. Your insights could:

...empower one more teen to start saving early.

...inspire one more young adult to invest in their future.

...encourage one more reader to make informed spending choices.

...support one more dreamer in securing a financially stable future.

To spread the joy and make a genuine impact, simply:

LEAVE A REVIEW RIGHT HERE:

https://www.amazon.com/dp/B0CZJ6NK1G/

I'm beyond excited to guide you through more eye-opening financial strategies in the future, follow me on Amazon to get updates. Trust me, the tactics, lessons, and strategies we're about to explore will change the game for you.

I'm beyond excited to guide you through more eye-opening financial strategies in the upcoming chapters. Trust me, the tactics, lessons, and strategies we're about to explore will change the game for you.

Heartfelt thanks for being a part of this journey. Now, let's dive back into our adventure.

Your guide and biggest supporter, Freddie Awuah-Gyasi

P.S. - Remember, sharing valuable knowledge makes you an invaluable resource to others. If you think this book can make a difference in someone's life, don't hesitate to pass it on.

Made in the USA
Coppell, TX
12 November 2024